PUSHING
Through

PUSHING
Through

Finding the Light in Every Lesson

NICOLE D. VICK

Contents

Acknowledgments

Writing this book has been quite a journey that I wouldn't trade for anything in the world. I am so grateful that I have the opportunity to share all the lessons I've learned in the first four decades of my life with you. I couldn't have done this work without the help of some amazing people:

To my daughter Andréa, who has taught me so much about who I am. Thank you for your unwavering support and encouragement. We grew up together; this book is just as much about you as it is about me. I love you.

To my mom and dad and my younger brother, who taught me so much and helped me to remember important moments while writing this book.

To the Fabulous SistaFriends of South LA: Nomsa Khalfani, Maisie Chin, Jackie Provost, Jameelah Powell, and Sonya Vasquez, thanks for being a sounding board for all these years and for helping me grow professionally and personally. I hope that I am as good of a friend to you all as you have been to me.

To all the professionals I've worked with over the last 15 years at the health department. I have learned so much from you all about public health, professionalism, and ambition. Thank you for introducing me to public health and sharing your passion with me. I would especially like to thank the staff in the South Los Angeles Regional Health Office.

To Tiffany Romo, whose words the day of that meeting at work lit a spark and compelled me to act, to write, to speak about the faces behind the numbers.

To my maternal great-grandparents, Tommie Lee Cross Simpkins and Rufus Simpkins, my maternal grandparents, Eddy Mae Cross Neal and Nathan Neal, and my paternal grandmother, Mary Lee Luckey. I stand on the mighty shoulders of my ancestors. I would not be here without the sacrifices they made. Thank you for all the lessons and the wisdom you shared with me

To Kim O'Hara, the person that helped me get everything that was inside of my head onto paper and helped me realize it was indeed possible for me to write a whole book. I appreciate your ability to help me see this through.

Foreword

by Senator Holly J. Mitchell

Nicole Vick's story of self-determination through the lens of a Black woman coming of age in South Central Los Angeles (yes, I called it South Central!) is one of both courage and fear, passion and agency. Her story and life experience are both familiar and unique.

I, too, had grandparents and great-grandparents who made South Central Los Angeles their home. From the Easter Parade along Central Avenue to the stories of the Jazz greats who made the Dunbar Hotel and Club Alabam historic destinations – these families worked hard to build a community and institutions that continue to struggle. From the work of the Black church, to the historic civil rights organizations, the non-profit sector, to government, we continue to search for the answers to our community's current yet persistent needs.

In reading Nicole's powerful accounts of family migration, teen parenting in Trojan-land and self-discovery, I am reminded of the many stories I have heard my entire life. The poignant difference is – Nicole did not just survive, she is thriving. Her storytelling is an important reminder to Black women that we have a collective responsibility to ourselves to save ourselves - first. Our battles with self-image, sexism, racism are toxic and yet through Nicole's life example, we can and do make it.

Her story is not merely a "girl makes good and leaves the community" account. Nor is it a depiction of a monolithic character who has come to the rescue of a community. Nicole clearly practices what she teaches (literally) every day, with a refreshing dose of transparency and humor. Not every autobiography will include such honesty and grit. She helps us to understand that our journeys are never really over, as she continues her personal quest to live healthier and happier in South Los Angeles.

Through Nicole's personal academic pursuits, to her years of teaching public health and the social determinants of health, she charts a path many of us should follow. A path where we each identify our own purpose, a calling if you will, that guides our investment in the future of our people, our community, our very own lives.

I applaud the blogging, public-transit riding Style Vicksen! Her story is quintessential Black Girl Magic…and yet it is a story that has just begun.

Introduction

'm a black woman born and raised in South Central LA. I was also a teen mom and then a single mom. I graduated from the prestigious University of Southern California with a master's degree. Yet none of these defining factors make me unique or different from the other black women that grew up in my neighborhood. What sets me apart, what sets any of us apart, are the stories and experiences that shape and mold us into who we are beyond the parameters of "the hood." The achievements, struggles, disappointments, lessons, and triumphs of my life have changed me to where my geographic locality should be almost insignificant. But it's not. I chose to have a profession in public health focusing on the exact issues in my neighborhood and county that have been around since before I was born.

Although my story may be different than yours, and the color of our skin a different hue, I speak for all women working hard in the inner city to raise children, maintain family, and find their sense of self. Survival alone is difficult and all consuming, but tribes and communities can be found. Women need to stop isolating in the shame of their condition and place themselves where they can be supported and encouraged.

I've spent almost two decades working to prevent disease and promote health in Los Angeles County. I had no idea that my life experiences and desire to help my community would both propel me into public health as a career choice and afford me the opportunity to look back at my life through a public health lens. This discipline has afforded me many opportunities to help people, which is all I ever really wanted to do with my life. I've helped residents live healthier lives by working with organizations on important public health topics like violence prevention, STD prevention, and infant mortality. I've helped students understand the importance of public health and guide them towards careers in public health during my decade-long teaching career. I've also led committees and commissions focused on improving community health.

Through all of this work, I started to notice that my voice and views were valid and needed to be heard. Although I am sure they exist, I have never met another single-parent teen mom with a master's degree who understood the issues in the community, spoke out about them AND still lived in the neighborhood. My voice and the way I saw the world had context in my workplace and field, in academia, and in my leadership roles. The time had come to share my thoughts with you all with the hope that women with similar experiences would be empowered to not only identify with my story, but to act to improve their lives and their communities as well. Communities that have been historically under resourced and also have long-standing generational health crises such as high rates of infant mortality, STDs, violence, unemployment, and low high school graduation rates.

Social and economic inequity permeates every aspect of our neighborhoods, from the underfunded schools to the abandoned storefronts that line the boulevards. Lack of opportunity fueled by disinvestment, structural racism, and oppression shapes every aspect of our lives from where we live, work, worship, and play, to what we eat. Women will be the ones to take the lead in making significant change in our inner cities. Our life history gives us the framework to create the tools to bring about change. We just need the encouragement and the motivation from our sisters, our friends, and colleagues to move us forward on an endeavor that seems relentless.

Structural racism is uncomfortable. Our government and society has been shaped to adversely affect minorities, particularly black women. The impacts of structural racism don't just impact our ability to progress economically. We internalize it, which negatively affects our health. When I talk about these issues, with students, colleagues, residents, and stakeholders, I make it clear that how one navigates the world and whether they are able to do so successfully can be impacted by structural racism and other forms of oppression like sexism. For example, a black woman's experience during pregnancy and delivery can be very different than that of her white counterparts. Her interactions with her physician, the quality of her prenatal care, her experiences during childbirth, and whether or not her questions or concerns are heard and addressed can all be negative simply based on her race. These negative experiences amount to more than just an unhappy and dissatisfied new mom; they can be life threatening. Add to that the already negative impact societal pressures have on the expectant black mother that can lead to premature delivery or infant or maternal death, and we have a recipe for disaster.

My public health colleagues and I work incredibly hard behind the scenes to keep everyone healthy. Public health is a social justice institution that aims to ensure that everyone has access to opportunities to live healthy lives. The focus is on prevention of disease and promotion of healthy behaviors, but the work to get there can be quite complex. Making sure that everyone gets a chance to live a healthy life means that resources need to be distributed equitably. This may mean that some people need more resources than others in order to gain that access such as increased wages, better access to health care, or better-quality schools

Growing up I didn't know about structural racism, oppression, or inequity beyond the requisite lessons on slavery, Jim Crow, and Martin Luther King, Jr. taught each year during black history month, but I was given messages very early and very often in the media, in social interactions, and in interactions with various institutions that I was not in the mainstream. When I entered graduate school and later the public health workforce, I understood that the marginalization of people that looked like me had very real implications. That truth is no excuse for women to back away from making the necessary demands on their community and institutions to offer them as much of a shot as anyone else to succeed in the world.

As a government employee and public health professor, I spend a tremendous amount of time studying, researching, and teaching about populations of people that have poor health. For twenty years I have answered the STD hotline, run programs focused on health equity, sat side by side in planning meetings with former gang members, and provided public health information to elected officials. In public health, if we do our jobs well, no one knows we exist. Some days we hardly get the needle to move, but we continue the work, day in and day out, to solve complex and multifaceted public health issues. We don't give up and continue to chip away.

Prologue

The Training

I received an email to attend an in-person racial equity training designed to help public health employees and staff from a number of community-based organizations understand the impact structural racism has on community health and to help us to think more strategically about how to integrate this information into our respective work. When the training was complete, participants would understand that the society we live in is racially structured, causing the disparities we see regarding race. It's not a "few bad apples" that are corrupting systems. It's not poverty that is causing the issue... it's the very core of this country's foundation that is the problem.

The topic wasn't new to me, as I had been exposed to it while working for the department for several years at a location just south of Watts.

However, on this particular day, the way the information was being examined was a bit different. As I walked into the training room, I wondered why it was being hosted in this space. The "training room" was an auditorium on the first floor of the building I worked in. The same room that, up until a few years ago, had ashtrays on the backs of the seats, a symbol of a bygone era when people could smoke inside. It was the irony of all ironies in a facility that housed public health staff. It seemed so odd to be having such a deep and sensitive conversation in this setting. The room did not foster discussion of the material presented or provide any intimacy. The training would be purely one-directional, with information being exchanged one way, from the facilitators to the staff in attendance. I had experienced this disconnect many times before, most recently when completing an online training module about child trafficking. It was very hard to process, and I felt left alone to wrestle with the uncomfortable feelings that came up with the heavy material. There were no discussion groups after the training, no email address or phone number to call to talk, absolutely nowhere to put those feelings. You just checked a box, "training complete", and moved on with the rest of the day.

I took a seat next to a friend of mine in the back of the auditorium. There were approximately one hundred people in the room, a mix of department staff and people that worked for other agencies across the county. Many were black or Latino, but I saw a few Asian and white people throughout the audience. The facilitators introduced themselves and began the training. At one point, they landed on a graph that showed black people fare worse in every single system in society than white people. Every single system: health, education, criminal justice, child and family services, and economic. Every single one. They used indicators such as death from diabetes, infant mortality, third-grade students reading below grade level, incarceration rates, number of children in foster care, children living two times below the poverty level, and unemployment. Long story short, to be black was to be a failure.

Throughout the presentation I experienced many "mouth open" moments. I found myself muttering "what the hell" several times at the information that was being shared.

I have always known I was a member of a group that suffers some of the worse health outcomes and fares the worst in every single system in society—employment, housing, education, and criminal justice. African Americans on a whole are perceived as violent, uneducated, unemployable, sexually irresponsible, and negligent. Their children are criminalized, often treated as adults. The women are considered angry, objectified, and their bodies politicized. Black people get sick at higher rates than whites and people of other races from diseases such as diabetes, heart disease, and cancer and die sooner than everyone else. In short, "my people," my neighbors, cousins, friends, in my community, are perceived as both dangerous, and in danger, and have been for many generations.

Yet, I was seeing this with a fresh perspective. I had it the worst of all. In this very room, in this very training, I was experiencing the disconnect between the facts and the feelings. The crux of what prevents the change that needs to be made so that the black community in Los Angeles County can thrive.

Two of the agency's executives were sitting near me. I could not hide my emotions, and why should I? The information shared was very important and a discussion for change was completely missed. In that moment, sitting in that room, I felt that my graduate level education, almost fifteen years of work experience, and the ability to understand these concepts was both a privilege and a burden. I felt the weight of the whole race of which I was a member. I cannot imagine anyone feeling okay with hearing that everyone that looks like you will ultimately suffer. The worse part about it was that the cause of the suffering was not an accident. It was not some unfortunate calamity that had befallen this group of people. The cause of the suffering was intentional and for the benefit of others.

In public health, we are being constantly asked to rethink our work so that those differences are acknowledged, understood, and taken into account when interacting with clients, and that day we were invited to better understand concepts behind our public health work, but the same courtesy we are asked to extend to our clients was not being extended to us. We continue to hear the same data, stated differently with not much context given, and without opportunity to debrief or unload how this information feels. I was sitting in a racial equity training learning about how important race and racism is when we think about the health of communities, and we weren't addressing the elephant in the room. We weren't talking about the impact these concepts have on employees who may be absorbing the same information in very different ways. We also weren't talking about the racism, both structural and interpersonal, that exists in the workplace. It's easy to forget that employees, as educated as they are, are often members of the very groups that are being discussed during the training. At the very least they are residents of the county we are dedicated to protect, sometimes living in the neighborhoods that are most impacted. I grew quite angry and sad sitting in the training. Why does it feel like black people always get the short end of the stick? The whole structure is completely broken, or maybe it isn't. Maybe the system is acting exactly like it was supposed to and it is our job to turn it on its head and build a new one.

I thought I knew everything about public health as an adjunct professor for ten years, as well as my previous work experience in South Los Angeles. I had seen the data, the charts, the graphs, the maps with the big red dots hovering over South Los Angeles. I've witnessed it with my own eyes doing the work on STD prevention, violence prevention, and infant mortality prevention in black and brown neighborhoods. The grim health facts for African Americans was not new to me.

I looked over at my friend and colleague, wondering if he felt as sad and angry as me. I wanted to stand up in that auditorium and say, "People that look like me are SUFFERING." My stomach hurt.

After the training, I knew that rather than hold all of what transpired in my thoughts, I would have to talk to other folks who understood. I rushed out the door to the bank of elevators and made my way back to my desk. I shared my frustration about how bad it felt to hear the harsh realities about people that look just like me via email with a small group of coworkers. The ladies I emailed had also attended the training and were similarly dismayed and left without any real solutions. One of my coworkers wrote something very profound. "The problem is that when they see numbers, we see faces," she typed.

She was absolutely correct. Public health folk rely heavily on data for many reasons: to determine where to focus public health programs, to measure whether or not the programs work, for funding, and for many other reasons. What's often lost is context. No one ever talks much about why the data is the way it is or who the people are that are being measured.

I thought about my family, my friends, my neighbors, the people I see walking up and down the street, the guys sitting in front of the liquor store, the kids walking to and from school. Indeed, these people have faces! They are much more than a chart or a graph. They are more than statistics. Their lives matter.

It's beyond stressful to be poor, black, and *female* in South Los Angeles. The chronic stress associated with living in communities impacted by violence, unemployment, and lack of resources is debilitating. While very rich with history and culture, not much wealth is present here. Many residents live at or below the poverty line and struggle to afford the basic necessities. South LA is a very complex community. I once heard someone say that South LA is more about a sense of identity and pride than it is about a specific location on a map. The many neighborhoods of the community, from Historic South Central to Leimert Park, Baldwin Hills, Florence Firestone, and Watts make up the rich tapestry of South LA. Some of the communities here are the poorest in the entire county. Many parts of South LA are also impacted by violence and trauma. There are also issues related to the shifting demographic of the area from black to brown, environmental racism, gentrification, and lack of employment opportunities. As a result, residents in parts of

South LA have the lowest life expectancy in the entire county and suffer from high rates of chronic and infectious disease.

The unfortunate part is that many of us internalize stress and don't even realize we're doing it. When we have to worry about what school we will send our children to so that they will be safe from harm and actually get a quality education, that adds stress to our lives. When we worry about allowing our children to go outside to play for fear of them being trafficked, harassed by the police, initiated into gangs, or being shot, that adds additional layers of stress. Add to that the unhealthy foods prevalent in our communities, the need to self-medicate in order to manage the trauma and stress from day to day, and the lack of mental health resources, and there is a perfect storm for a whole host of health and mental health conditions.

The training lit a fire in me. I thought deeply about what the information presented meant to me and to everyone in my community. Although the concepts weren't new to me, I had a sense of urgency to share this information with as many people as I could. I shared with my colleagues at work, the undergraduate class I was teaching at the time, and anyone else who would listen. My experiences in that training inspired me to find ways to speak publicly on this very important issue. In early 2018 I submitted a pitch for TEDx Occidental College and in April of that year I gave my first talk on the significance of my lived and professional experience along with my work in social justice and how it shapes almost everything I do from my thoughts and actions to the way I teach. I also spoke about the importance of diversity and representation in academia and in the workplace. The training and the TEDx talk helped me realize that I needed to sit down and put everything that was on my mind about these very important concepts in writing.

That training was uncomfortable and downright painful. I could have easily shut down, discouraged and defeated by the enormity of it all. Instead it lit a fire under me. The training forced me to move, to use my voice to bring awareness and change to those that crossed my path. I knew I had to tell my story, to share what I know so that others will be compelled to make change in themselves and their communities as well.

Chapter One

South Central: My History

Many people view Los Angeles as the mecca of openness and freedom. It's a place of imagination, of creativity, of luxury and opulence. Los Angeles has another side not seen. Segregation. Natives know how segregated Los Angeles is and what areas are acceptable and unacceptable for certain people to step foot. New arrivals to the area may not know of the history behind why some neighborhoods are consistently poor and under resourced. For locals, the social divide has been ever present. Everyone knows that the area just south of the 10 freeway near the 110 freeway is one that you move through quickly on the way to somewhere else or visit for very specific purposes. Either you get in there and get out quickly, or you avoid it altogether. What is forgotten is that there are entire communities of people there, living their lives much like everyone else except they live under the exhausting weight of poverty, racism, and lack of opportunity. I grew up in one of those communities and have seen the resilience, perseverance, and vibrancy of the residents despite the many factors that impact our community like violence, poverty, and unemployment. The disinvestment and outright neglect of the community I grew up in caused all of these problems to grow exponentially. One of the touchpoints of my childhood was the 1992 civil unrest that occurred in South Los Angeles. I was in eighth grade on April 29, 1992, when the four policemen who beat Rodney King were acquitted. It was one of the scariest times of my life. I couldn't understand why the policemen were able to escape punishment. The beating was recorded, and it was obvious to the world that the police were wrong. At fourteen years old, I understood that law enforcement could hurt people that look like me. The other scary part was seeing the community rise up in anger and consume itself. My family and I watched on television as familiar businesses were looted and burned to the ground. There was footage of store owners armed with guns protecting their properties. Why were people burning down their own neighborhood, our neighborhood? The scene was upsetting to witness. Why didn't they head west and wreak havoc on the more affluent part of town? As I got older, I better saw the dynamics at play. The community had just been told that what happens to black lives doesn't matter. Despite clear evidence that Rodney King was wrongfully beaten by the police, because he was black there would be no justice for him or for us. Black people in the community were tired of having to swallow that maltreatment, so the anger and the sadness and the trauma erupted like a giant volcano right there on Florence and Normandie and flowed like hot lava through the city streets. There would be no venturing west to wreak havoc on anything. Police didn't stop the destruction of South LA, but I suspect they would have quickly killed any notion of unrest on the Westside. When my family finally ventured outside several days after the unrest began to get groceries at Ralphs on La Brea and Rodeo, the National Guard were out front with big guns monitoring shoppers as they came and went. The civil unrest and the aftermath left an indelible mark on the community. Many businesses that were burned down didn't return, and the community was neglected and ignored for many years. Outsiders were left with negative impressions of the community and the people who lived here. They didn't understand the context, or the historical abuses inflicted on the community by law enforcement; they just knew to avoid the area at all costs. It was an unfortunate situation that the community is still trying to heal from decades later.

Despite the negative perception of the communities of South Central in the years following the civil unrest, life continued. Community treasures such as the Watts Towers and the California African American Museum continued to stand tall as beacons of hope in those early years after the unrest and continue to represent an important cultural history in South Central Los Angeles and the greater metropolitan area. In fact, all of Los Angeles is very rich with architectural and cultural history. Old statues and turn-of-the-century buildings give me pause and make me wonder about the people that inspired them and how life was "back then." I routinely Google landmarks that I run across while driving through Los Angeles, scrolling through my phone with one hand while trying to read up on the origins of a statue, structure, or neighborhood. As a child, I used to sit for hours studying old Thomas Guides, tracing familiar streets in my community, making note of the changes that have occurred over time. I would trace the streets of my neighborhood with my fingers as I wondered who Mr. Crenshaw and Mr. Slauson were. I looked for Martin Luther King, Jr Blvd., only to discover that its original name was Santa Barbara Avenue until it was changed in 1983 when I was five years old. I marveled at how wide South Broadway was as it ran through South Los Angeles, with old theaters and large storefronts long ago repurposed as churches and discount stores. I embrace Los Angeles as my city, my home, and the foundation for the ideals that shape me in my work and personal life. I remain awed by the history of my community and take every opportunity to learn and understand where the city started so that I can better understand what kind of city Los Angeles will be in the future. We all should be working to make our corner of Los Angeles a healthier place for everyone to thrive.

My love for history was inspired by my maternal grandparents and great-grandparents. Before my brother was born, I was the only child in my mother's immediate family. My mother's older sister didn't have children, and my cousins on my dad's side didn't live very close, so I was the only young person among my very small immediate family. I was talked to less like a baby and more like a grown-up. I was considered a full part of the family unit and therefore exposed to a lot of real-world experiences such as the failing health of my aging grandparents and great- grandparents and conversations about real estate and property that my family owned. I also had the whole terrain of their homes and history to explore on my own without competition with other kids.

My great-grandfather, Rufus Simpkins, was a portly, loud, and vivacious man from Rolling Fork, Mississippi. He owned a Shell Station on Central Avenue with his business partner Mr. Gower and had a real estate company called 40 Acres and a Mule many decades before I was born. He and his business partner built the apartment buildings on West 35th Street that I lived in with my mom and dad and younger brother. These buildings, along with other properties my great-grandparents owned, were the source of the generational wealth that my family benefitted from, and that is so elusive to many black families in this country. My mother lived there with her parents and older sister decades before. At home, he'd let me sit behind his great big wood desk and show me how to write checks. I had no idea at the time, but he was grooming me for success. I have seen photographs of my great-grandparents standing in front of the Shell station, looking proud and quite fashionable. There are photographs of my grandfather working at the station as well.

My great-grandmother, Tommie Simpkins, was a cosmetologist and makeup artist. She was born in Tennessee in 1898 and was raised in Oklahoma with her sisters. She married at nineteen and had one daughter, my grandmother Eddye Mae. The marriage ended, and in 1931 she came to Los Angeles with my grandmother and married Rufus in 1936. She had a salon called Colonial Beauty for many years on Historic South Central Avenue when that area was a haven for black folk on the West Coast. I was impressed with her entrepreneurial spirit during a time when blacks were not always afforded the opportunity to flourish. I am very sure that the love of beauty products and makeup that my aunt, my daughter, and I have comes from my great-grandmother. It's almost like it runs through our veins.

Like most black folk of her generation, my great-grandmother understood the value of a college education. She would often ask me what I wanted to be when I grew up. More specifically, she would ask me if I was going to go to college. When I replied "yes" like a good great-grandchild was supposed to, she'd say, "Good, then you'll be Dr. Vick!" I still feel compelled, over thirty years later, to get a doctorate degree at some point so that I will indeed be Dr. Vick.

My great-grandparents' travel west was part of the "Great Migration" that millions of black folks made from the South to the East Coast, Midwest, and the West Coast between 1916 and 1970. The neighborhood where my great-grandparents arrived in the 1930s, now called Historic South Central, has changed so much over the years. Once predominantly African American, Latino families now reside in the densely populated neighborhoods. Main thoroughfares feature storefronts with signs in Spanish: *panaderia, iglesia, carniceria, lavanderia.* Street vendors selling *elote,* tamales, tacos, and fresh fruit line the avenues. Despite the shift in demographics, many remnants of the rich black history of the community remain, such as the Dunbar Hotel, which housed prominent African American musicians and celebrities who were not allowed to stay in Hollywood or Beverly Hills.

I enjoyed spending time with my great-grandparents and grandparents. Their homes were like castles, with rooms full of all sorts of treasures to explore and discover. I spent a lot of time with them in my formative years of six through ten, developing the foundation under my identity as a black girl. They connected me to my history in ways that I didn't see happening with my other friends in school. When I went to hang out with my friends at home, I didn't see black and white photos of their family members or old *Ebony* and *Jet* magazines.

My great-grandparents' home was old school. There were wood-paneled walls in the den, shag carpet in the living room, and mirrored, gold-veined walls in the dining room. Old furniture and knick-knacks from another time and place filled the rooms. The best places in the house were the living room and the den. There were easily hundreds of issues of *Ebony* and *Jet* magazines spanning decades. I loved looking at all the photos and advertisements and seeing men and women dressed up, smiling and happy. Those magazines were a step back in time and showed me the best of black culture and society.

My grandparents' house was also a place I loved to visit. When my parents would take me, the first place I'd run to was the living room. The space was just off the main entrance to the home and was full of beautiful Asian decor. There was a huge white sectional in one corner of the room, with a black lacquered coffee table in front of it, a big black baby grand piano on the other side of the room, and a tumbled stone fireplace. The built-in shelves next to the fireplace contained knick-knacks with Asian influence, but there was one thing on those shelves that I always gravitated towards: a series of white and green World Book Encyclopedias from the 1950s lined up in alphabetical order. The information contained in those books had to be about thirty years old at the time, but I would voraciously read through each book like it was brand new.

My favorite one contained costumes from ancient times through the 1950s as well as traditional clothing from all over the world. I would sit in a bright orange chair covered in plastic (to protect it, of course) and turn the gold-lined pages. I loved looking at all the colorful and ornate costumes and how different they were from each other. I also really loved what was considered the "current" fashion from the 1940s through 1950s. The lines of the clothing were so beautiful, and the full skirts and shirtwaist dresses were from a different time and place. My love of fashion started right then and there.

If I wasn't fixated on the encyclopedias, I was at the piano practicing my lesson for the week. My mother signed me up for weekly lessons with an older lady named Ms. Roach. She was a stern old lady who lived in an old messy house near Jefferson and Crenshaw. I thought she was so mean! Every week I went for my piano lessons and afterwards I'd go to my grandparents' home to practice what I had learned. Ms. Roach's piano was old and small, with worn out keys. My grandparent's piano was big, beautiful, shiny, and black. It was fun to sit on the piano bench and practice songs out of my red piano lesson book. It was even more fun to open the piano bench and look through my aunt's old sheet music from her youth. She had the same piano teacher that I had growing up and played very well. During the family gatherings my aunt would play the piano; her graceful fingers would dance across the keys while mine clumsily searched for Middle C. I loved my auntie Janet and looked up to her. Growing up she was the coolest adult I knew. She always had great stories to tell and introduced me to new and exciting foods that I'd never tried before. She taught me about fashion, colors, and makeup. I would spend the night with her often and loved looking through all the clothes and shoes and makeup in her home. There was always so much stuff in her house, which made it part of the fun of being there. She loved Mae West and Betty Boop and had their posters all over the house. We'd watch Rocky and Bullwinkle cartoons while working on a puzzle or sharing a meal. She was someone I aspired to be and, in some ways, I am very much like her with my curly hair, my big smile, and my commitment to public service. I never did get as good as she was on the piano though. I have found through conversations with many other women that they too shared in this experience of the piano teacher and the passed down sheet music.

The other place I loved to peruse at my grandparents' home was the cabinet below the shelf that held the encyclopedias. This is where all the old family photos were. I loved looking at the mostly black and white photos of my grandparents. They were always dressed up like they were going to a party. In every photo my grandmother always had a beautiful dress on and looked so well put together with her nicely coiffed hair. There were also pictures of my aunt in her debutante ball dress and her very 1960s bouffant hairstyle. There were also amazing photos of my grandfather during his time in the military. He was enlisted in 1942, a year after the bombing of Pearl Harbor. He was very rugged, smoking with fellow military, or relaxing, presumably after a hard day's work. There were also photos of naked women kept in an old photo album. I think they were showgirls or pinup girls. At first, I was shocked to see them! How could they be here in the house with my grandmother here? Why weren't they hidden away so that I wouldn't find them? But over time I became intrigued with them as well and would look at them again and again. The women were beautiful and wore feathers or other sorts of costume as if in a show of some sort. They were very curvy and quite beautiful.

This glimpse into my family's history filled me with pride for my family, my community, myself, and a sense of purpose. There is something to be said about knowing where you come from and who came before you, on whose shoulders you stand. The many pictures and artifacts in both homes were constant reminders for me and very important given that many black people have no real clue about their true origins other than they are descendants of West Africans that more than likely came to this country as slaves. Their names, language, and religion stolen hundreds of years ago.

I looked up to my grandfather, Nathan Neal. I spent most of my time with him when I went to visit my grandparents. He's the one that taught me what "gesundheit" meant and about a faraway city called Reykjavik. He was so smart and knowledgeable and always had great tidbits of information to share. We would drive around to Buddha Market in either their white Lincoln Continental listening to jazz music or his tricked out blue Mustang with the funny sounding "ahooga" horn. He would also pick me up from school in his Mustang. I was with him and Grandma a lot while my parents worked. He worked at my great-grandfather's old Shell station pumping gas and repairing cars. He met my grandmother while on the job, and in 1941, they were married.

Most importantly, I saw my grandfather take care of his family. He not only maintained the house, took care of the cars, and other household things considered "manly," he also did most of the cooking. I cannot recall a time that I saw my grandmother lift a finger to cook anything during my childhood.

My grandfather retired from LA City Fire Department in 1978, the same year I was born. Years later I would see a photo of him in the African American firefighter museum. I was at a cycling event called Ciclavia that closes city streets and allows cyclists and pedestrians to have fun exploring communities across LA. This particular day, Ciclavia was rolling through Central Avenue, right near the community where my family lived generations ago. I noticed the museum and walked inside to look around, hoping to get some insight into what his experience was like during his time with LA Fire. I walked into the converted fire station and began to look at all the photos of the black firefighters. I stopped in front of one photo and an immediate feeling of familiarity swept over me. I was looking at a photo of my grandfather! The caption mentioned he was sitting on a water cannon. It looked like a huge truck with a giant water hose on top. The museum official explained to me the amount of prejudice and discrimination my grandfather endured while on the job. I had heard similar stories from my aunt while I was growing up and the impact the incidents had on my grandfather and on the family. The museum official told me that my grandfather integrated the fire station at the Los Angeles International airport during

9

his career. I was impressed but not surprised. It appears public service and leadership runs in the family.

My grandmother, Eddye Mae, was slender and had warm brown skin. She walked with a limp and with one hand forever clenched in a fist due to a stroke she had shortly after I was born. She smoked Camel cigarettes and always wore a perfectly coiffed wig and a flowy caftan. When I visited, we'd watch TV in her bedroom, talk about school, and play a game or two of Backgammon on the bed. I loved perusing the many bottles of perfume she had. Scents with names like Youth Dew and White Shoulders lined the black lacquered dresser in her room.

My mother often shared bits and pieces of her experience with my grandmother growing up. One that surprised me was her struggle with alcoholism. My grandmother did not drink by the time I arrived on the scene, but this wasn't the case when my mother and my aunt were growing up. My mother relayed a story once of coming from school and being very thirsty, finding a bottle of what looked like ice-cold water in the freezer, and taking a huge gulp only to find out it wasn't water at all. Growing up my mom never quite knew which version of my grandmother would be home when she arrived from school.

At the time, I didn't quite understand the impact of her drinking on my mother's childhood, but later I would come to understand the impact of substance use disorder on both the person afflicted and their extended family, and how prevalent alcohol and drug abuse was in the black community. Many people in low-income communities who are under the crushing stress of poverty are victims of violence or some other trauma, or suffer from mental health issues use drugs to attempt to cope, to self-medicate. It is their attempt to mask or erase the feelings that are bothering them. In the inner city, alcohol and cigarettes are much more available with liquor stores at almost every corner.

It is well documented that harder drugs like crack cocaine were more or less dropped off into black communities, wreaking havoc on communities and destroying families. The current response to the heroin drug epidemic of this generation is very different from the "war on drugs" that happened as a result of the crack epidemic. Part of me wants to believe it's because we have a much better understanding of addiction. Part of me knows that the response is different because the people afflicted are different. Black people suffering from drug addiction during the crack epidemic were not afforded the same grace and understanding as those in the current clutches of the opioid epidemic, who are predominantly white. The impacts of these decisions have permanently changed the landscape of many black communities across the country, including South Los Angeles. Families have been broken up due to incarceration or death, and the lack of substance abuse treatment facilities means that many who were addicted to crack years ago are unable to effectively reintegrate into society, so they remain unemployed, homeless, or behind bars.

I did not, by any means, grow up poor. We were also not rich, but having relatively well-off grand and great-grandparents had its benefits. I existed in this very interesting duality, straddling the line between opportunity and lack. My parents didn't hold high-paying jobs, so I didn't grow up with name brand clothes or shoes. My parents never had new cars, and we lived in an apartment until I got to junior high school. However, I attended parochial school, and the apartment and homes we lived in were made possible by my maternal great-grandparents. Both my maternal grandparents and great-grandparents lived minutes away from each other in a community that is often referred to as "Black Beverly Hills." The communities of View Park and Windsor Hills are full of very beautiful large homes that have expansive views of the downtown LA skyline. Many prominent African Americans such as the former mayor of Los Angeles, Tom Bradley, called the area home. The streets are tree lined and quiet, an amazing contrast to the loud and gritty city life down the hill.

By the time I came along, my grandmother and grandfather were in their mid-sixties and my great-grandparents were eighty. Of course, I knew they were old, but I really had no concept or idea of how old they really were. I knew about the love and care they provided, but it was not until I was much older that I realized other families didn't have the opportunities my elders afforded me. I was able to go to the parochial school because of them. My grandparents and great-grandparents would pick me up from school while my parents worked and provide me a safe space in their home to play or explore, keeping me out of trouble. A strong family support system is very important in providing a layer of protection around children as they grow up. I often hear people lament that the sense of family and community is not the same as it was a generation or two ago. This may be true. Many families cannot afford for one parent to stay home while the other works. In many families, there is only one parent anyway, so this isn't an option.

When I grew up, my grandparents and great-grandparents were retired. Retirement comes much later for many grandparents these days, especially if they are raising their grandchildren, which happens more often than people think. It is so much easier for children to fall through the cracks when there isn't a strong support system in place. Behavior issues or poor school performance often get missed or overlooked because the parents are doing their best to keep the family housed and the lights on. Parents are often caught in a terrible bind, having to work very hard to provide basic needs and not having the time to dedicate to their children in a way that nurtures them. Society has done a terrible job of prioritizing children by creating an economic reality where people have to work long hours or multiple jobs just to make ends meet. It's not fair to the family and it hurts our children the most.

Besides the help with my schooling and housing, my great-grandparents owned a boat and a mobile home at Lake Mead just outside of Las Vegas, Nevada. So these road trips became our small family vacations. We would visit during the summer and enjoy the huge two-bedroom, two-bathroom home. I would sit with my great-grandfather outside as he smoked a pipe in the warm summer evening, the crickets all around making their loud noise as the day ended. Every summer we would pack up the old woodgrain station wagon with a huge cooler full of snacks and drinks and make the four-hour drive to the lake. Sometimes one of my cousins would go with us, but most of the time it would just be me, my parents, and later my younger brother. My grandfather would also get us tickets to Disneyland every year in September for my birthday. They were an employee benefit from his previous employment as a firefighter. Even then tickets were quite expensive, but we got to go and have fun on all the rides. My favorites were Pirates of the Caribbean and It's a Small World.

The other benefit of having my grandparents around had huge impacts well after they were gone and is often elusive for many people of color for many reasons: generational wealth. My great-grandparents owned properties that were passed down to my mother, my brother, and I. Unfortunately, mismanagement of those properties caused them all to be sold or lost to foreclosure. Although my great-grandparents did a great job of accumulating assets, what they failed to do was pass their knowledge down to my parents. This lack of knowledge sharing caused several missteps that our family could not recover from. The upside was that we had properties to sell to avoid financial ruin, but it would have been much better to have kept those properties in the family, especially since those properties have increased tremendously in value. Our family is now forever priced out of View Park and Leimert Park, communities that have increased exponentially in value and are becoming gentrified. Fortunately, I was able to take what I learned from my great-grandparents and ensure my family's financial security after I'm gone by purchasing property. I now own two income properties thanks to the foresight of my great-grandparents and have made it a goal to acquire additional ones over time.

My years with my grands and great-grands are a sharp contrast to what I see today. Many people are waiting to have children or are choosing not to have them at all. At the same time, despite increased life expectancy due to many improvements in public health, people are living much shorter lives. In 1997, my almost one-hundred-year-old great-grandmother got to meet her great-great-granddaughter and spend three months with her before she died. We just aren't seeing that type of longevity these days for many people, especially in the black community due to the impacts of racism and inequality on our health.

Although my immediate family didn't have an enormous amount of resources, my grand and great-grandparents were an important part of my upbringing and offered financial stability, a sense of history and awareness of self, and role models that I looked up to. It would seem that the positive trajectory of my life was already set in stone. I just had to show up and do the work needed to get successfully from childhood to college, and all would be well, right? I paint such a vivid picture of my family history, the roots, the pride, and my deep connection to South Central to show that even I struggled to find my place within the societal conditions that existed in my community. Despite having amazing odds in my favor, I was still affected by poor societal infrastructure and social conditions in my neighborhood. My life would take a significant and unexpected turn between my graduation from high school and my graduation from college. What happened in those few short years could have changed the trajectory of my life entirely. I can only imagine what transpired for those far less lucky than me.

Chapter Two

South Central: My Home

M any factors play a part in the health of communities. The most significant are what are called the social determinants of health. Where we live, are educated, work, worship, and play have a direct influence on how healthy or unhealthy we become and how long we live. Racism, specifically structural racism, plays a role as well. Structural racism can block access to the social determinants of health, adding another barrier to health, financial stability, and quality of life for black people. These concepts can seem very abstract and nebulous, but the implications are very real. The inability to access these basic resources can lead to high burden of disease and early death.

One very real example is the evidence of structural racism in the housing sector. Housing is a social determinant of health. Simply put, housing provides shelter and safety from the elements and a sense of security, stability, privacy and control. Housing also makes significant contributions to health and well-being, it's a place to rest and relax, and is often a source of identity for many.

When my great-grandparents arrived in Los Angeles in the 1920s–30s, they could not live wherever they chose to. Although Los Angeles was much more liberal than the deep South at the time, there were restrictive covenants and other types of de facto segregation that kept them and their black neighbors confined to Historic South Central Avenue. The community thrived for many years, but over time it became densely populated as more and more black families moved to Los Angeles during the Great Migration. Starved of economic opportunity and jobs, the community started to deteriorate. Residents who could afford to move wanted to move to Compton, West Adams, and other neighborhoods that were predominantly white at the time. They were often met with violence and very strong opposition. Once the restrictive covenants were removed, black families began to integrate those neighborhoods. Decades after my grands and great-grands arrived in Historic South Central, they would move west to Jefferson Park, then to Leimert Park, and finally View Park. Their white neighbors left those neighborhoods and moved to the suburbs to avoid living with black people. The irony is that white families are returning to the communities they abandoned a generation ago because reasonably priced housing is becoming harder to find in Los Angeles. Poorer residents are getting pushed out of neighborhoods that were overlooked and neglected for years. These were the same neighborhoods that my classmates and friends lived in while I was growing up. Neighborhoods that lacked resources and jobs. Where something as commonplace as a grocery store was nonexistent. Where gang violence was common. Once again, I existed in this strange duality, removed from all the realities of living in South Central while my grands and great-grands were alive. I spent so much time in their homes, with the views of the city skyline, and the tree-lined streets. There was no graffiti or gangs that I was aware of. I was a part of the community and yet removed from it.

There is a lot of stress and anxiety associated with being poor. The connection between stress and health is very clear. The more chronic stress a person is subjected to, the more likely they are to experience chronic illness and shortened lifespan. Poverty also inhibits a person's ability to navigate through life successfully. If you've ever tried to adopt a healthy diet or live in a better neighborhood with a very small income, you will understand where I am coming from. Your choices are almost always limited by what is immediately available to you. The easiest example of this phenomenon is food availability in South Central Los Angeles.

I was a chubby kid. I loved food, and my extended family, especially my great-grandfather, gave me lots of it. There was an abundance of food, but not much in the way of variety when it came to fruits and vegetables. I didn't have the best eating habits growing up, but it wasn't their fault. It wasn't anyone's fault. There wasn't this level of awareness about food like there is today. I don't think they realized the mistakes being made. My great-grandfather just wanted me to be happy. When I visited, he offered me huge bowls of chocolate or strawberry Mocha Mix ice cream. What kid would say no? Bowls of candy and unshelled pecans were around the house, which I loved to crack open with a nutcracker and eat by the handful. My great-grandfather was from the South, and like many black folk of his generation, food was love. There was no such thing as saying "no" to that bowl of Mocha Mix ice cream, and so portion control or a balanced diet was not on my radar growing up.

Today, with what I know about nutrition and its effects on children's health and their success rates in school, I view the neighborhood I grew up in as a food swamp, devoid of options to buy fresh produce and overrun with fast food establishments, liquor stores, and small corner stores. There was plenty of food, just not enough fresh food options to offset the abundance of fast food. We didn't know better as kids; we ate what tasted good to us and what was available. We didn't know that the food we were eating would likely set us up for high blood pressure and diabetes, especially if we were already genetically predisposed.

I lived directly across from Trinity Baptist, a very large Baptist church. Just west of the church, across the large dirt field used as the church parking lot, was Roy's Market, a mini market that sold meat, produce, packaged food, and candy. We would walk across the lot to Roy's Market to pick up sliced bologna, hot links, chili bricks, iceberg lettuce, bread, or any other items we needed. When I got older, I was allowed to walk there alone to pick up groceries for my family or walk with my little brother or friends to get candy. The store was very convenient, but the food was very poor quality. There were often roaches and other vermin running around among the packaged food. Sometimes we'd find evidence of those pests in the food! But we kept shopping there; it was the closest store and that was all we had. Our grocery store choices were shaped by our immediate environment.

Just north of Roy's Market was Burger Palace, the hamburger stand where my dad took me to eat the day my mom went to the hospital to deliver my younger brother in December of 1983. Burger Palace sold hamburgers and burritos so greasy that orange-colored oil would drip down your hand when eating. Meals were served with a side of fries and a soda. There was no "side salad" at Burger Palace.

Two blocks west of Burger Palace, across the street from the public library, was "the candy store." It was a tiny storefront stocked full of all types of candy. Now and Later, candy bars, *tamarindo*, marzipan, *saladitos*, Chick-O-Sticks, Botan Rice Candy, snow cones, and anything else you could imagine was there. The store was run by a sweet older lady, and her grandson helped ring up purchases. We would stop there on the way home from the library to get our treats.

The only "real" grocery store close to us was Notrica's 32nd Street Market, right across the street from USC in the University Village. UV, as it was called, was run-down and full of cheap stores, an amazing yet sad-looking international food court, a very small movie theater, and a laundromat, an interesting contrast to the prestige of USC, which was five minutes east of us. 32nd Street Market was a place overflowing with people when we would go grocery shopping on the weekends. The sights, sounds, and smells were overwhelming. Women that looked like me but spoke fluent Spanish or with a thick Jamaican accent crowded the meat counter, buying meat, chicken feet, beef brains, or seafood. Entire families were in the produce aisle picking through the poor-quality fruits and vegetables, looking for the best out of the bunch. *Veladoras*, religious candles with saints on them, lined the shelves on one aisle, and *chicharrones* and *manteca* lined other shelves. We'd buy Springfield brand products such as soda and canned food because it was cheaper than the name brand versions. The store was run-down, but we kept going every week. There were no other options in our neighborhood. Such was the food environment in my corner of South Los Angeles in the 1980s. That shopping center has since been torn down and now has a Target, a Trader Joe's, a gym, and a myriad of upscale food options. No remnants of the old facility remain, the landscape of the community forever changed by the ever-looming footprint of USC and its desire to accommodate their growing and more demanding student population. Although the new stores would seem to be a benefit to the community, there is an unspoken yet very clear understanding that the new amenities are for the benefit of the USC students and not the working-class residents that live nearby.

At home, my mother cooked all our meals, and I thought everyone ate Hamburger Helper, Shake N' Bake, Rice-A-Roni, hot links, fried chicken, pork chops, or salmon croquettes for dinner. A lot of our foods were fried in Crisco or vegetable oil. Vegetables were served covered in butter and Lawry's Seasoned Salt. Iceberg lettuce and Wish-Bone brand Italian or French dressing were the only ingredients in our salad. We washed everything down with Kool-Aid, Cactus Cooler, Sunny Delight, or Tang. No one I knew drank "regular water." In fact, we all thought plain water tasted terrible, our palates were so accustomed to sugary soda and punch. Like any other child growing up in South Los

Angeles, I enjoyed my fair share of Blow Pops, Skittles, Cool Ranch Doritos, and other treats full of sugar and empty calories that were available in abundance. The ice cream trucks cruising the neighborhood were also a source of fun and tasty treats.

While there weren't many food options, there was an abundance of liquor stores. These stores sell alcohol, cigarettes (sometimes illegally as singles), and loads of sugary and salty junk food.

A healthy relationship with food was not fostered in school either. School lunches contained baloney sandwiches, chips, and a Capri Sun or Squeeze-It to wash it down. Apples or oranges placed in my lunch box were left uneaten. I once got in trouble for eating a Hostess apple pie given to us during a field trip to the Weber factory because I chose it over the apple in my lunch pail. The pie was quickly discarded by my mother after I was admonished for my poor decision. In public school, the lunches were also terrible but reflected the tastes that we all had developed for processed food. Microwaved burritos, nachos made with processed cheese sauce, and greasy pizza were popular in junior high school. There seemed to be no oversight or programs to ensure the food was healthy. Convenience and cost appeared to be the main driver of the types of food served instead of health.

I often ate more than I was supposed to, like my internal "full" indicator was broken. "Finish everything on your plate" was the moniker of good health and abundance, fostering a borderline compulsion. There was no such thing as wasting food in our home. We were never without food, but I was an emotional eater, eating for comfort or out of boredom. I would eat three or four pieces of pizza while my classmates in school ate one or two slices, continuing to eat well after my stomach was full.

Although I wasn't the biggest child in elementary school, my weight had become a concern for my family. My mother fed me strawberry-flavored Slim Fast starting in third or fourth grade. The thick shake was my breakfast every morning before school. We'd put a scoop in a bottle, pour in the milk, add a raw egg "for more protein" my mom said, and shake it up. It tasted terrible. My mother meant well and was doing what she thought was best for me. She was often ridiculed for her weight as a child and didn't want me to suffer the same fate. Unfortunately, the extra focus on my weight set me up for many years of low body image and always seeking a fast solution, versus a more body-positive, whole body approach. In high school, I modified my food intake drastically and managed to lose quite a few pounds. Lunchables became my daily lunch, and I didn't eat much else. By the time I graduated from high school, I was very thin, almost too thin. In my high school prom photo, I had on a pretty cream-colored satin gown with lace at the shoulders, my hair full of curls. I was very skinny, and my face was just shy of looking gaunt. Disordered eating was in play, but I was skinny, and for the first time, I felt pretty. I had a boyfriend who was one of the most popular guys in school, my grades were good, and I had a lot of friends. What more could I ask for?

As I grew into adulthood, instead of a balanced diet and exercise, I turned to dieting and plastic surgery to fit an unrealistic standard. I incorrectly associated fat with "bad" and skinny with "good." I sincerely believed that my life would improve if I lost weight.

My parents also tried to get me exercise. They signed me up for softball at Ladera Little League when I was in elementary school. I went to the first day of practice and was put through a series of drills. I was not interested in softball, and it was very clear that there were many kids who were way more active and experienced. All the kids were sorted out, and the kids who were beginners were put on the Red Farm Team or the Blue Farm Team. All the good players got placed on more advanced teams. I don't think I ever caught or hit the ball. I was afraid of getting hit by the ball and wasn't very coordinated. I was so glad when Little League was over. I hated it.

As I got older and my weight climbed, I tried many different "quick fix solutions" to conform to society's weight standard instead of addressing the feelings inside of not being good enough, of insecurity that would not change no matter what weight I was. Being uncomfortable in your own skin can be the source of many issues, especially for women. I had serious body image issues that started way back in elementary school, and no one was helping me process the feelings associated with those issues. I had no body-positive role models and knew no women happy to be in their larger shape. As far as I knew, everyone was either slender or trying to get there by any means necessary. Unfortunately, the conversation hasn't changed much for young girls who still struggle with accepting their bodies in a society that constantly tells them what an ideal body should look like. Thankfully, there are many more examples of diverse body types, but the pressure to confirm to an unrealistic ideal persists. Body positivity would come into my world as an adult, and now I understand the importance of loving who you are in your skin to have the greatest impact in all areas of your life.

Another institution that has impacts on the health and well-being of communities, both positive and negative depending on who you ask, is religion. No matter where you stand religiously, having a spiritual foundation lends to good health. A regular spiritual practice can be important in developing and maintaining social networks, which are important in managing stress and other difficulties. Traditionally, in church. Socializing with people who share common interests and goals can be extremely rewarding and affirming. People who pray regularly or have a place to worship often have shorter recovery times following an illness. Some religions have specific mandates regarding health and well-being, such as not eating pork or veganism, and many have a focus on important social justice issues, such as taking care of the poor and the elderly, which are all important to public health. Because of this, many public health organizations work with faith-based organizations to share health information or to gather people around important public health issues such as violence prevention.

In the black community, not holding traditional religious beliefs is considered blasphemy. People will question your blackness, whether or not your "black card" should be revoked if you don't attend church on a regular basis. Religion is central to almost everything in our community, and church is seen as the foundation of our culture as blacks in America and has been since well before we arrived in the United States over 400 years ago. To be black and anything other than a Christian is an anomaly. Agnosticism and atheism are unheard of and are typically met with hostility or defensiveness. I have many friends who grew up in very strong church families and have a very strong relationship with God, but I had a different experience with religion growing up that made me feel very different from my friends and colleagues. When I was little, my parents would send me to Sunday school at Trinity Baptist Church, the big white church across the street from our apartment on 35th Street. My mom would wake me up, feed me breakfast, get me dressed, and send me out the door to walk across the street to Sunday school by myself. My parents weren't at service in the sanctuary while I was learning; they were at home! I suppose in their mind they were doing right by me by making sure I was going and learning about the Bible, but it felt weird to be there without them. I had no social connection to the larger church community, so I was an island. I missed out on the benefit of community that a church home offers. The other kids in the Sunday school class already knew each other because their families were already members of the church, which made socialization very awkward for me. When Sunday school was over, they would leave together and walk to the sanctuary to find their parents and sit through church service. I would just make my way back across the street to my home. I never made any lasting friendships with any of the kids there

23

because I only saw them once a week for maybe an hour. After a while, I disliked going and eventually my mother stopped sending me.

In elementary school, I attended a parochial school attached to a small church in South Los Angeles. The pastor's wife was the principal of the school and we saw the pastor quite often because he led the church that the school was affiliated with. He would come visit us in the classrooms and was genuinely interested in our lives and what we were learning. It was clear that he loved us all. He knew all our names, and no one ever felt slighted or forgotten.

Every Wednesday morning we'd file out of our classrooms and head to chapel, which was held in the sanctuary. At the front of the sanctuary, above the altar, was a huge mural of white Jesus made out of small colorful tiles. I would hide from his gaze whenever I had to walk through the sanctuary from the classroom to visit the front office. As a child, I was always freaked out at pictures that had eyes that followed you around the room, and the gaze of Jesus in long flowing robes and a halo over his head was no different. The pews, light brown and made of wood, lined each side of the main aisle. There were beautiful stained-glass windows that lined both sides of the building. To the left of the altar was the choir stand, a piano, and a huge church organ.

During my time there we had two music teachers. Ms. Gallagher was an older white woman and the last of the white folks that attended the small Lutheran church. We learned hymns that I can still sing word for word almost four decades later. Songs with titles like "Beautiful Savior" and "His Name is Wonderful." Songs that I learned years later that not a lot of other black folks know because they're not sung in Pentecostal churches. Coates, a talented pianist who taught special education students as his day job, was the music teacher and also gave students piano lessons. During chapel we'd sing, listen to a short sermon, and recite passages such as the Apostles' Creed, which I still know by heart.

While I have not attended church in almost twenty years, my world view and interest in other cultures lends to my curiosity about different religious practices. I've enjoyed learning about Islam from a coworker fasting during Ramadan and on one occasion cried while watching a documentary about Islam. The explanation of the preparation before prayer and the sounds of the prayers overwhelmed me, and I had a deep and profound respect for what I was watching, even though I couldn't understand any of the words. I've visited Buddhist temples in the San Gabriel Valley and Bangkok and walked the grounds observing all the beautiful and ornate facilities and statues, in awe of the beauty and reverence displayed.

Religion can provide a wonderful foundation by which people live fulfilling lives. It provides purpose, kinship, and support to many and can be a helpful reminder that we're not alone in this world. Religion also provides structure and guidelines to live by for those who desire it. You don't have to be Christian to incorporate spirituality into your life; you just have to be in tune with yourself and your place in the world. To me, spirituality is about respect for self and for everything around us. It's also about the connection between us and all living things.

Other people of color also have similar difficulties with navigating successfully through our country's social structures and often have similar struggles with important cultural mainstays like religion and food. Latinos, who often live side by side with blacks in South Los Angeles, are victims of the same structural racism that impacts African Americans. Unfortunately, we are often pitted against each other in the struggle for resources and respect. Language and cultural barriers add to the dissention and separation. The irony is that we struggle in the same underfunded schools, live in the same under-resourced communities impacted with violence and crime, and fight for more well-paying jobs. We both want safe and healthy communities to raise families. Blacks and Latinos, specifically Mexicans, have been in Los Angeles since the beginning, when forty-four *pobladores* arrived in 1781. Because our histories are shared in many respects, it would seem to follow that we would suffer from many of the same poor health outcomes, and for the most part this is true. However, Latino Americans tend to have health outcomes that are equal to or better than their white counterparts, even though their income and education levels are lower. This phenomenon is called the Latino Paradox. No one knows for sure why this is the case, but it is very interesting given that higher educational attainment and higher income are social determinants linked to better health.

Other issues that dominate low-income neighborhoods are access to check cashing and payday loan businesses, keeping residents outside of the traditional banking system and trapping them in a cycle of high-interest payday loans. Communities are also full of industries that emit toxins and pollute air. Homes and schools are within feet of oil drilling sites, waste dumps, freeways, or battery recycling factories, exposing families to toxic chemicals in the air, water, and soil.

My experiences growing up in South Central, for better or for worse, shaped me. The spaces where I was born, lived, went to school, worked, worshipped, and played held such huge implications on my future. I understand today the importance of creating communities that nurture instead of vilify. We all have a responsibility to work to make our communities safer, healthier, and vibrant for the next generation.

Chapter Three

Say What About Education?

My college students sometimes ask why students of color, particularly black students, have such low high school graduation rates if it's widely known that education is a protective factor—a ticket out of the hood, so to speak. They wonder why so many students drop out or fail to take school seriously. I explain to them that the quality of schools is a major factor in student retention. Schools in black communities are usually old, run-down, and in very poor condition from years of subpar funding. Textbooks are often outdated, and sometimes there aren't enough of them to go around. Routinely, teachers are not given the proper training and support to work with students who need a lot of support. School easily becomes a place that students prefer to avoid altogether. After all, if they feel like no one really cares, why would they show up? I also talk about students getting "pushed out" of school (as opposed to "dropping out"). This happens when schools are unwelcoming or uncaring and/or have zero tolerance policies that fail to recognize extenuating circumstances or the subtleties of life. Students are often criminalized in inner-city schools. School police are on campuses in full force, along with metal detectors and other methods of penalizing students, placing students squarely into the school-to-prison pipeline. There is also the factor of how well a person can navigate a system that was ultimately not created for them to succeed in in the first place. I sincerely believe that many of the systems that exist in today's society were not created for black and brown people at all.

Structural racism also plays an integral role. Policies that promoted segregation and were structurally racist such as "separate but equal" had huge impacts on black students' ability to attain quality education. These policies began to be struck down around 1954 but existed well into the 1970s. Imagine attending a separate school that was nowhere close to being equal regarding resources. How is a student supposed to graduate, succeed economically, and have a quality standard of living? It may seem as though we have moved past those discriminatory practices, but they persist. Research shows that many school systems today are more segregated than they were decades ago. Also, implicit bias and other types of discrimination impact how black students are treated in the classroom. For example, data have shown that black students and students with disabilities are suspended at higher rates than other students. Dress codes that prohibit braids and afros, traditionally worn by black students, were starting to make the news a few years ago. All of these policies, whether intentionally oppressive or not, make it clear to black students and their families that they are not welcome participants in the educational system. It's really a miracle that any inner-city kids graduate at all, the odds are stacked against them.

What saves many students is their resiliency, the capacity to keep coming back and pushing through after continually being pushed down and out, and their overwhelming desire to succeed. Black students make it with the dedication and determination of their families. I will never believe that black children and their parents are less interested in education than others. It's simply not true. I remind my students that low graduation rates are not a reflection of the students' intelligence and willingness to learn. Students' inability to graduate from school is a stark reflection on the education system's inability to provide adequate resources to communities with the most need. Many of our kids are not having their potential realized and shaped in a way that brings out the best in them. So many of our systems and institutions are failing black children. They are not, and have never been, the problem. If a system is failing its customers, fix the system, don't blame the customers. It is a huge loss of human capital not just for black communities, but for everyone.

"Making it" should not only be reserved for the few kids that either get a lucky break, play sports, or are lucky enough to have strong family structures. Every child should have the opportunity to do well. It's amazing that so little investment is put into the educational system, and yet society is surprised when the outcomes are less than stellar.

Community support of schools, in all forms, is integral to student success. Parents are the most important resource for schools. Parent participation in the education of their children can be challenging due to work and other competing priorities, but their presence and input is valuable. Parents often set the standards and expectations for their children's experience in school and can (and have) successfully advocate for policy change. Parents also get the chance to give back by participating in after-school activities, in-school activities such as career day, and in other ways to show support. Unfortunately, in many communities, black parents are seen as hostile and adversarial by teachers and the school administrators and are treated as such without any regard for or understanding of their own experiences with school, the types of trauma they have endured, or their current living situation. Local businesses, community- and faith-based organizations, and other agencies are also important to the success of schools. Many of these organizations provide funding or services to fill in gaps left by lack of district funding. They are also often met with resistance due to school district bureaucracy or other barriers. Schools and school districts must find ways to better incorporate these organizations so that schools are better supported.

One great example of the sense of community happened during my sixth grade year. Every year, the sixth graders got to go on a trip to Washington D.C. and New York for a whole week. It was a big deal, and everyone looked forward to going. I was a bit scared. I had never been on a plane before and I didn't think my parents could afford it. I don't recall there being an explicit conversation with my parents about me going or not, but my impression was that it wasn't going to happen. Every Friday, the school had a hot dog sale to raise money for the trip. From what I understand, the parents were supposed to pay for airfare and accommodations and the funds from the hot dog sales were for souvenirs, meals, and other incidentals. All I remember is that once it was made clear to the principal that I wasn't going, she made sure that enough money was raised to cover my entire trip. I was not made to feel different or bad about our family's financial status. My "scholarship" was not publicly disclosed (although some of the kids did ask me about it), and I was able to fly on a plane for the first time in my life. I got to visit the Statue of Liberty and we saw *The Phantom of the Opera* and all the great monuments in Washington D.C. I was so grateful for the opportunity to travel and see another part of the country. It was a big deal for an eleven-year-old black girl from South Los Angeles.

For junior high, I got my local "public school experience." During the last few months of elementary school, my classmates were excited about moving on to junior high school. Students were talking about which schools they were going to and their plans for the summer. At some point the fact that I was going to the public school Audubon Junior High for seventh grade was put out there. I think the teachers were worried about me going to such a big school. So much so that one day my sixth grade teacher, Mr. Williams, sat with our class in the parish hall and read a story about my future school that was published in the August 1988 issue of *Ebony* magazine. It was a story about how the school had improved academically, gang activity had been eliminated, and how the school received many accolades for improvements in student achievement under the leadership of then-principal Gene McCallum. While he read the article, several students snickered. Mr. Williams did not mess around. He stopped mid-sentence and admonished the class in his strong Jamaican accent, reminding them that this was not a joke and that one of the students in the class would be attending that school. In his own way, he was trying to reassure me that the school was okay while also trying to squash any of the rumors or negative talk that might come from the students.

My first days at Audubon Junior High in the fall of 1990, I was completely overwhelmed. There were so many students! I was coming from a school where there were about one hundred students total and this school easily had over a thousand students. I was now in a public school where I could finally wear what I wanted, which was a blessing and a curse because I still struggled with body image. I picked my clothes out of the JC Penney and Sears catalog women's section since I had long outgrown the "girl's plus" section. Plus-size clothes in the early '90s were mostly ugly floral prints, baggy silhouettes, and horrible colors. The trendy plus-size clothing lines that exist now for young people did not exist. Plus-size clothes at that time were very matronly and designed for adult women. The other kids at school wore bright Cross Colours and Karl Kani and other cool clothes that were popular during that time. Not only were those clothes too expensive for my family, but they didn't quite fit my body the way they fit everyone else. The trend at the time was baggy, loose-fitting, brightly colored clothes, and there wasn't anything like that in my size at the stores where I shopped. One day I finally was able to get a pair of bright yellow Cross Colours jeans. I was so excited and made sure to wear them to school. I was standing outside of one of the classrooms between periods, happy in my yellow jeans, finally feeling like one of the crowd.

"Why do your jeans fit you like that?" said a girl pointing to my hips. The jeans were very snug across my hips, not loose and baggy like the other kids. I looked down at myself, acutely aware of my body in a way that was very uncomfortable.

"Because she has wide hips!" my friend said admonishingly.

My head dropped in shame. It feels terrible when you don't fit in. Currently it's a great thing to be different, to be original, to push back against societal norms. When I was growing up it was harder to be different, especially when there was no one that looked like you to look up to.

What scared me most about public schooling was the cussing and the fighting! I also was scared by the talk of gangs. Whatever the *Ebony* article had said about there not being gangs on campus back in that 1988 article was not quite true because by the time I arrived two years later, there were definitely gangs on campus. If it wasn't the students themselves, it was their older siblings or relatives who had the connection. I'd see them driving around the campus after school, sound systems blaring, or catch graffiti or tags on my classmates' book covers. Of course, I knew gangs existed, but I had minimal exposure to any of the lingo or discussion about gangs. As kids we just knew not to wear too much red or blue and to not wear British Knights tennis shoes because BK stood for "blood killer." Remember, I grew up in a family of mostly adults. I had cousins on my father's side of the family, but I didn't see them very often. I only played with one or two kids on the block. In many ways I was very sheltered, so a lot of the conversation about "sets" and gang territory was new to me. Thankfully I was able to avoid being immersed in gang culture. I was seen as the "good kid" and the nerd, so students generally left me alone. I was not bullied or subjected to the peer pressure to conform that affected so many other students in my school. Because I was one of the smart kids, I was placed in a program for gifted students, which also kept me away from a lot of trouble and provided me with additional support and resources to succeed, but junior high was indeed an interesting time.

Even though I was in "public school," I had an outstanding group of teachers. Mrs. Bright was an amazing teacher who related so well to all the students and was like a mother to us all. She was a black woman from the community (she attended Crenshaw High School, a very popular local high school, around the time that my mother did in the early '70s) and talked to us like we mattered. Ms. Miles was the soft-spoken science teacher who made learning fun. It wasn't a big deal to me that she was a black female science teacher at the time, but I realize how significant that is now. One of the Spanish teachers at our school was a black woman. I had never seen a bilingual African American person before. My math teacher, Ms. Broussard, was a no-nonsense woman who made sure we knew our stuff! Ms. May was another no-nonsense woman. She taught English and often allowed us to sit with her during lunch time. She also facilitated the Academic Pentathlon team, which Lisa Woo and I participated in with a small group of other students. We got to wear satiny green Audubon jackets and travel to another school to participate in the academic competition. These black women represented possibility and aspiration for me and my classmates. Also, we were able to relate to them. They looked like our mothers, our aunts, our families. They set a standard for us to meet. When we met it, they celebrated with us; when we didn't, they helped us work through it.

The school was primarily African American, but there were students from many different cultures. I had a Chinese American friend, Lisa Woo, whom I lost contact with and recently reconnected with after twenty-three years. She was really cool, and we got along so well. She lived a mile or two away from school in a duplex with her parents, who spoke almost no English, and her younger brother. Despite the cultural differences, we were good friends for a very long time. Her parents would cook us food and we learned a lot from each other. One day in Ms. Bright's class we had to create a family tree and share it with the class. I could only go back as far as my great-grandparents, but Lisa produced an elaborate family tree that went back many generations, written in Chinese. It was amazing to see. For another assignment in Ms. Bright's class we had to pick a hero, write about them, and share our essay with the class. My civic-minded self was already evolving, so I picked Yvonne Braithwaite Burke, the first black woman member of the Board of Supervisors for Los Angeles County. Lisa picked her mother. As she began to talk about how hard her mom worked and the sacrifices she made, she began to cry. It made me realize that everyone is going through something, that her parents wanted for their children the very same things my parents wanted for me, and that seeing and understanding someone else's perspective is valuable, not only to me but to the other person. To be seen and acknowledged is very important. When I reconnected with Lisa, she remembered that day clearly as we sat and reminisced about our time in school together.

One of the most interesting occurrences happened in ninth grade when a girl in my class got pregnant. I was shocked! I knew what teen pregnancy was, but I just couldn't fathom being pregnant at fourteen. I was still very much a kid, and yet she seemed so much more mature than I was, so much surer of herself. She was one of the most popular kids in our class. The students loved her. She was very pretty and seemed to have an old soul. She had a beautiful singing voice and was just one of those kinds of people that you just wanted to be around. One thing I admired was that she stayed in school the entire time she was pregnant, despite opposition from administration. She had a right to be educated, so she stayed in class as long as she could.

My mom and dad were worried about what my experience would be at an even larger public school like Crenshaw High, the local school in our neighborhood, so they plopped me back into a parochial school in Inglewood with about one hundred students for high school. I was sad because I had made a lot of great friends at Audubon that I would ultimately lose contact with because I didn't get to go to Crenshaw. I also really wanted to go there because my mother had gone there many years before, and I thought it was a really cool school. To this day I see the difference in the relationships that my junior high school friends have with each other as they moved on to high school and into adulthood. I have been fortunate to keep in touch with quite a few of them thanks to social media, but I was only able to maintain close relationships with very few.

Both my elementary and high schools were Lutheran schools. The upside to returning to parochial school was being reacquainted with many of the friends I had in elementary school, and the smaller class size allowed the teachers and administrators to know the students and care about what happened to them. They also had a better/closer relationship with parents. For parents who cared about a religious/spiritual aspect, those teachings were provided to the kids. The rigor was not there for the super nerdy kids like me—arriving ready to take Spanish 3 and there was no Spanish 3 class available—but on the whole most of the kids got what they needed academically.

I took sign language instead, which was a great class, but I firmly believe I would be fluent in Spanish if I were given the opportunity to take Spanish 3 in high school. I was also a bit more advanced in math than everyone else, and by my senior year I was trying to take calculus via a correspondence course because no one on staff could teach me. I ended up abandoning the course completely because I didn't understand the content and didn't have the appropriate help to figure it out.

My social life in high school was average. I had quite a few friends, some from elementary school, and some were new friends. I was on the cheerleading squad and got along with all my teachers. I enjoyed my newfound independence gained as a result of having my driver's license. I was able to go to and from school by myself and hang out with friends. We had homecoming events, a winter formal, and prom, and we had a great time!

Although my parents thought that parochial high school would protect me from teen pregnancy, drugs, alcohol, and other negative behaviors that happen in public school, it didn't quite turn out the way I think they thought it would. After all, kids will be kids, regardless of what school they go to. Hormones don't magically turn off in the parochial school setting. During my senior year I started dating a very handsome guy and became sexually active at age sixteen. We spent a lot of time together. He was smart, witty, a singer, and a musician. It felt great to be found attractive and desirable for the first time. I had never experienced that before as an overweight kid. High school was a time when I was starting to understand who I was in relationship to men. I was not very confident in myself, and I overcompensated by being over accommodating. I would do his homework and other things that I probably shouldn't have done like skip class. I was naïve and wanted the attention and affection and did whatever I needed to do to get it. This was the beginning of a negative relationship with men that lasted well into my thirties.

Finally, the time came to leave high school and move on to the next phase of my life. Graduation was amazing. Because of all my hard work, I was class salutatorian, the number two student out of a class of thirty-five. I wrote an amazing speech based on Matthew 5:14–16:

> "You are the light of the world. A city set on a hill cannot be hidden. Nor do people light a lamp and put it under a basket, but on a stand, and it gives light to all in the house. In the same way, let your light shine before

others, so that they may see your good works and give
glory to your Father who is in heaven."

My boyfriend wrote a song for the ceremony, which we performed
together in front of everyone in the church auditorium. The title of
the song was appropriate: "Nothing Lasts Forever." Looking back, the
chorus was a bit strange given the occasion, but hey, we were in high
school so we went with it:

"Nothing, nothing lasts forever.

Sometimes it has to end and you must cry."

I was excited to leave high school and move on with the next part of
my life. I was on my way to college and I was excited. While I had no
idea my life would be more aligned with my pregnant classmate back in
ninth grade, I firmly believe that my school experience and my family
support system laid a great foundation for me to be able to move past
any obstacles that crossed my path later in life.

To improve education outcomes in my community, I'd like to see
more black teachers in the classroom, especially black male teachers.
Studies show that black students succeed when black teachers are in the
classroom and that black male students do especially well when black
male teachers are in the classroom. At my small parochial elementary
school of about 100 students, I had all black teachers, two of whom were
men. I remember all of their names like it was yesterday: Ms. Oates,
Ms. Phillips, Ms. Parker, Ms. Washington, Mr. Manzanares, and Mr.
Williams. They were all black. My time in elementary school was so
beneficial! Everyone was like family. Sure, there were the typical things
that happened like bullying and disagreements and fighting, but they
were dealt with quickly and with love and care. Looking back, we were
well taken care of and the sense of community was very strong. Most
importantly we were held accountable for our actions both inside the
classroom and outside on the playground. If you messed up in any way

you would feel like crap and as if you'd let everyone down. That same sense of accountability continued on to middle school with the black teachers I had. I benefitted greatly from the sense of community and pride that was cultivated by my teachers during my formative years. I imagine the reason that the number of black teachers has decreased is due to low salaries, poor recruitment, and the difficult job of teaching in low-income communities, but more has to be done. The importance and relevance of a young child of any race seeing a black teacher, especially a male, as a leader can do so much in erasing prevailing stereotypes about black men as well as affirming black students in the classroom.

While there are many things wrong with the current educational system in black and brown communities like South Central, such as lack of funding and policies that funnel children down the school-to-prison pipeline, positive change is happening. Restorative justice programs provide opportunities for conflict between students to be resolved in a way that does not harshly penalize students. School districts are re-examining zero tolerance policies that often were very unforgiving and disproportionately impacted black and brown students. Schools are also training teachers on important topics like racism and implicit bias to help them treat their students more equitably. We have a long way to go, but I have hope that folks like me who grew up in the community can continue to speak out about what we have seen and foster change.

Chapter Four

An Unexpected Challenge

applied to one of the most prestigious universities in the country, the University of Southern California, as a biomedical engineering major. There was no career counselor at my high school to give me any guidance, and my parents didn't really know much about selecting college majors to help me, so I went with a nice career with potential for an impressive paycheck. I had absolutely no idea what biomedical engineering was. I still don't know, to be perfectly honest. The decision wasn't based on any of my strengths or interests and was definitely a testament to the "I don't know what the hell I'm doing" soundtrack playing in the back of my mind at the time. My only interest in science or engineering in high school was dissecting a frog in biology or creating some concoction that boiled over in chemistry class back in high school. I figured that not many black women would be biomedical engineering majors, so I applied with the hopes that declaring biomedical engineering would make it easier to get accepted.

I grew up less than two miles from USC, so when that large acceptance envelope addressed to me arrived at my home in April 1996, I was excited! The place that was the backdrop of my entire childhood was now within my reach. When I was a child, our family went grocery shopping across the street from campus at the 32nd Street Market. My junior high school graduation was held at Bovard Auditorium, right in the center of campus. I wore a beautiful white dress with a pleated skirt that day with my hair full of spiral curls. As my family and I arrived on campus that summer day in 1993, I marveled at how big the campus was and how important and stately the buildings looked. I would soon enter those same buildings as a college student. I was excited and a bit scared.

Five seconds into the introductory engineering classes at USC's summer "bridge" program for minority students, I knew I had made a big mistake with this biomedical engineering thing! I couldn't get into the content at all, but I was conflicted. I was having so much fun meeting new people, including my new roommate Vanessa, the first Latina I ever met who didn't speak Spanish, but I didn't want to go to any of the sessions that were being offered by the summer bridge program. In a way, I didn't really see any other option but to finish the program. I had to stick this out. I had made it all the way to USC, and now was not the time to backtrack or complain.

Despite my issues with my major and the summer bridge program, I enjoyed my brief time on campus. I felt like a "real" college student and a grown-up, just like the college kids on *A Different World*, my favorite television show growing up. I was a mere fifteen minutes from home living at Fluor Tower on the north side of campus, but I felt like I was really on my own. I made new friends, explored the campus, ate the tasty college food, and hung out in the dorms. I was at the school of my dreams and I had a super cute boyfriend, I was happy! My social life was amazing, but I couldn't say the same thing about my education. The uncertainty so early on scared me.

I finished out my crazy summer bridge program and began my first semester of college at the end of August. College was an interesting time and place for me. In high school I was very smart. I was class salutatorian, the smart girl who was going places. I didn't have to study to get good grades. I quickly grasped new concepts and was naturally curious and inquisitive. I realized that being one of the smartest kids in a graduating class of thirty-five students from an inner-city parochial school doesn't mean a damn thing at a large school like USC where there are thousands of students from across the country and all over the world who went to schools better resourced and staffed, and were from families with more money and more opportunity. I was a teeny tiny fish in the middle of the ocean, and I was completely overwhelmed.

To add to it, I felt out of place. USC is a PWI, a predominantly white institution. The 100-year-old campus featured buildings named after wealthy people who had either donated money to the university or were past presidents of the institution. Inside the buildings are paintings or photographs of faculty, donors, staff, and other people of importance to the university and the various schools throughout. They were almost always white and male. I had only black teachers until junior high school and even then, a good number of them were black. At USC, most of my professors were white men.

The student body was relatively diverse, but the mainstream population was white. It was odd to sit in class with students that I couldn't identify with. It was one of the very few times in my life that I felt less than, like I didn't deserve to be there. I was feeling a strange mix of insecurity, fear, and unfamiliarity, despite the fact that I had submitted an application and done the work to get good grades just like everyone. I had earned my way there fair and square. There was no free ride, no scholarship, no handout. My tuition was paid with a mishmash of grants and loans; some of those loans I'm still paying twenty years later. It's one thing to not feel prepared for college, and quite another to feel as though the college was not intended for you. That feeling of not belonging never really went away until many years after graduation after I had reached a certain degree of experience in my professional career and was asked to come back again and again to speak to current students about my expertise in public health.

I intend to always make a difference when I return to my alma mater and share my experiences in school and the trajectory in my profession. There could be a student sitting there feeling as lost as I did.

Institutions have a responsibility to make sure students from a variety of backgrounds feel welcome on their campus. As a black teen from South Central, the welcome mat wasn't put out for me when I stepped foot on campus. Navigating college when no one else in your family has been there can be very difficult. No one can give advice or understand your worries or fears. They are just so glad to see that you made it, and the rest of the journey is left to you to figure out. Colleges and universities should find new and innovative ways to support students who are pregnant and parenting and who have other extenuating circumstances beyond providing family housing for students with spouses and children. Students who are in the same situation I was in are more likely to drop out but are the very ones who stand to benefit the most if they have the support necessary to succeed. What is needed are support groups, counseling, and referrals to relevant services for students and their families.

While I was smart enough to avoid remedial courses—the classes that freshmen had to take when their math or other skills weren't quite ready for college-level instruction—I was confused and bewildered most of the time. Science classes were my biggest struggle. There were concepts, ideas, and information that I had never heard before that some students had learned in high school. I realized that in high school we barely scraped the surface and it put me at a huge disadvantage. In biology class, the professor was lecturing about some aspect of the periodic table that I had never heard before. I turned to my classmate.

"What is he talking about?" I asked.

"You didn't learn this in high school?" she whispered back

I was truly lost. My family was very supportive, but I'm not sure they understood what I was experiencing. They had done their job to get me this far, and it was up to me to figure it all out. They had no frame of reference by which to guide me. I was on my own.

I jumped from major to major. From biomedical engineering, to pharmacy, to nursing. I took chemistry and biology in the same semester despite being advised not to do so, and I paid royally for that mistake. I got a D in biology and had to use Freshman Forgiveness for chemistry to erase a failing grade. I thought it was super cool to skin a cat in anatomy class but couldn't focus long enough to learn the various body parts required in class. I was in trouble, in serious danger of being put on academic probation or even dropping out.

Thankfully, there were programs to help new students. I am forever grateful to the Black Student Union, the Center for Black Cultural and Student Affairs, and other organizations on campus that offered mentoring and other resources for me. I attended weekly mentoring sessions hosted by the Black Student Union and facilitated by black upperclassmen. I could ask them any questions I had and get support and advice. Because of these services, I was eventually able to find my footing and succeed.

To make some extra money, I took a job at Cafe '84, one of the cafeteria-style restaurants on campus. I could have gotten a job doing administrative work in one of the departments on campus or as a lab assistant. There were many work study opportunities, but I simply felt more comfortable working in food service. It was easy work that didn't require much thought. The place looked like it was from the 1980s. Everything was dated and drab. There was a hamburger and fries station, a pizza and pasta station, a Chinese food station, a salad bar, and a dessert station. The food was pretty good, the place just looked crappy. They updated it about a year after I started, but at the time it was a sad sight.

I was quickly hired and placed at the ice cream and milkshake station. I made banana splits, milkshakes, ice cream cones, and all sorts of cool things. The job was fun, and I made lots of friends. Grace, Rosa, and Candelaria were cashiers who worked there and were so nice to me. They weren't students working to help pay for tuition or for spending money; this was their full-time job. I identified more with them than the students. They were from the community while most of my classmates were not, so we had plenty to talk about, from the schools their kids attended to local happenings in the neighborhood. They would ask me about school and family life. I felt like a member of the family and not just a student worker. Our conversations highlighted the many roles I played at that time. I was student and community resident. We talked about the increasing tension between the residents and the increasing number of students who had started to move off campus due to the increasing need for student housing. There were still many black and Latino residents in the predominantly low-income neighborhoods surrounding USC, and some property owners were removing their long-term tenants to rent to students at much higher prices. The displacement was not going unnoticed and put the university in a bad light as not being a good neighbor to the community. I was able to understand the concern my coworkers had because I was raised in the community, but I also understood what was happening in a much broader sense because of the topics I was studying in school.

During my time at Cafe '84 I rotated to some of the different stations. At one point I was placed at the cash register to ring up students' food purchases. To be responsible for the register was a big deal to me at the time, and I welcomed the responsibility. Something strange started to happen as I rang up students' food. Whenever a student came to my line with something from the pizza/pasta station, my stomach would churn when the smell of tomato sauce wafted up to my nose. It got so bad that I would have to hold my breath when students came to my line

44

with pasta or any type of tomato-based food. I had no idea what was going on because up until that point, pizza and pasta were favorites of mine. I wasn't sure what it was, but it wasn't fun at all.

It was a crisp October day in 1996 when I went to the student health center. I hadn't been feeling well for quite some time and I decided to finally go and get checked out. I was seen by a wonderful doctor. I explained to her that I hadn't seen my period in a while and that I was often nauseated, especially when I was anywhere near tomato sauce. It was getting harder and harder to work the register at work with all the food smells. She was calm and reassuring and suggested that I have a pelvic exam. She told me she would be able to feel if "something was in there" and that if that was the case, she'd send me for a pregnancy test to confirm.

I got undressed and laid on the exam table.

"Yep, there's something in there," she said as I felt her fingers moving around. "But let's get a pregnancy test done just to be sure!"

This can't be happening. I might be pregnant? My heart sank.

I headed to the lab, where a nurse stuck me five times before she found a vein. A few minutes later I saw the doctor again and she told me the news. I was pregnant.

Up until that point I didn't think I could even get pregnant. I have no idea why I thought this. I had no medical condition that would prevent a pregnancy. I was of child-bearing age, and I was having sex, so it was a bit silly to think that I couldn't have children. I was in denial. But there was no denying this!

After hearing the news my mind was spinning: How would I tell my parents? What would they say? How would I manage school? What was I going to do? The rest of the visit was a blur. We attempted to figure out how far along I was and came up with ten weeks based on an educated guess as to the first day of my last period.

I left the health center and called my boyfriend on a pay phone outside of the building.

"Hi, Daddy!" I said when he picked up the phone. I wasn't one to beat around the bush.

He was in shock and didn't believe me right away. Our biggest hurdle to date was fast approaching. We would have to tell our parents, and they would not be happy about any of it.

I was this smart and studious kid, but I ended up pregnant at eighteen. I am grateful for my daughter, but with proper sex education, I may not have had to navigate college with a baby.

While there were several factors that led to my condition, there are three main issues that are directly linked. First, there was no conversation about sex in my family. I did not feel comfortable discussing sex, reproductive health, or protection with my mother. She would probably disagree, but the nature of our relationship didn't lend itself to being open about such touchy topics. She never said, "I don't want to talk about sex" or "just don't come home pregnant" like some parents say; we just never talked about it. Many parents don't. They worry that if they talk to their children about sex their kids will interpret it as permission to be sexually active, which is not true. When parents avoid talking to teens about sex, it is a missed opportunity for them to share their expectations about healthy relationships, provide accurate information about their bodies, and provide resources so that they are safe.

The lack of comprehensive sex education in the schools is another missed opportunity. When I was in junior high, the class watched a video on sex and reproduction, and in high school any education around sex was biblically focused, so talk about sex was focused solely on having children after marriage because teenagers shouldn't be having sex.

My low self-esteem largely contributed to my inability to negotiate consistent condom use, but frankly, condoms were not very accessible in my community. My boyfriend and I would go to the drugstore to try and buy condoms and they would be locked up in a cabinet that could only be opened by a clerk. We were young and already feeling unsure about being sexually active; the fear of being judged or turned away trying to buy condoms was very real and overwhelming. It was much easier to not bother with them at all. We had similar concerns with trying to access birth control. We couldn't figure out how to enter the health care system to get birth control, so we didn't. The thought of having to ask a clinician for help was so intimidating. We didn't know if we would be judged or ridiculed, so we steered clear. We encountered so many barriers: facilities with weird business hours that didn't accommodate our school schedules, cold and uninviting staff in facilities that looked like prisons with plexiglass separating us from the staff, and the overall feeling that young people just weren't welcome. Many adults will probably read this and say that we shouldn't have been having sex if we couldn't figure out how to protect ourselves. That may be true, but our feelings and desires for each other far outweighed any rational thought about the issue. The sexual health field failed us in many ways. Society failed us.

Normalizing condom use and STD testing, erasing the stigma surrounding discussions about sex, and creating more youth-friendly STD testing and treatment services would go a long way in improving the sexual health of our youth. Young people will not be deterred from doing what they want to, so there shouldn't be any barriers in making sure they are safe and have the correct resources to protect themselves. They wouldn't end up with children too young, too early, and in college like I did.

I wrestled with finding the right time and place to tell my family about my pregnancy. I was sure that they would all be so disappointed in me. I was the oldest daughter, the smart one, the one who followed all the rules and never got in trouble. And now I was pregnant at eighteen years old. I just knew I'd be in big trouble.

The thought of my mother's reaction scared me the most. I feared her judgment and disappointment more than anyone else. She already disliked my boyfriend and thought he was a bad influence on me, so being pregnant added fuel to the fire and confirmed her initial feelings. Strangely enough I didn't worry so much about my dad's opinion. He's pretty even tempered and has always been that way for the most part. My mother is the more expressive one. The one who often wears her heart on her sleeve and doesn't mince words. The thought of telling her made my stomach hurt.

Although I was in college, I still lived fifteen minutes away at home (Fluor Tower had just been for the summer program), and at this point in my life, home was my great-grandparents' house in View Park. Our family moved there to take care of my great-grandmother who was in her nineties at the time. USC is very expensive and there was no money for tuition, let alone a college dorm. Since I was still part of the family like in high school, we would do laundry and go grocery shopping together. Therefore, the grocery store turned out to be the perfect place to tell my mom about my pregnancy. She couldn't harm me in front of all those people. There would be too many witnesses, so this was the safest place to confess. On grocery day we piled into the family car and headed to Ladera Heights. Our family had graduated from 32nd Street Market in our old neighborhood to the Ralphs in this more affluent community. The facilities were cleaner, and the produce was much better. We parked, walked in the store, grabbed a shopping cart, and began to pick out our groceries.

I slipped away to look for the prenatal vitamins and selected a bottle that I thought would work best for me. I headed back over to my mother and placed the vitamins in the shopping cart. Honestly, I had no idea how this was going to play out. Was I was hoping she wouldn't see them right away? I don't know. I put them in the cart. She almost immediately picked them up, read the bottle, and looked over me.

"Why do you need these?" she said with concern in her voice. She was not angry or upset. She just asked the question straight out as if she was genuinely confused.

I started to cry. "I'm pregnant," I said through my tears.

I waited for a reaction. I waited for her to freak out, yell, turn red, something.

"Don't cry, it's okay," she said, and gave me a hug.

I was very surprised at her reaction. She seemed very happy, which wasn't what I was expecting. I was glad that I wasn't met with anger or judgment.

We went home and my mother told my dad, my younger brother, and my great-grandmother, whom my mother was taking care of. I was so worried about my mother's reaction that I had not considered anyone else's feelings. My father seemed to process it well, although I never really asked him about it.

My brother's reaction shocked me. When my mom broke the news, my younger brother got up from where he was sitting and without a word walked right out the front door. Knowing my brother, he was disappointed, mad, sad, and probably not happy with my boyfriend. He has always been protective of the family, and I had let him down. We never talked about that day, but he eventually came back home, and life went on.

Very early on, ending the pregnancy came up with my mom. My mother pretty much told me, "Well, if I would have done the same thing, you wouldn't be here."

At the time, I accepted that statement to mean that if she hadn't considered it when she was pregnant, then I shouldn't either.

Everything became a thousand times harder almost immediately after I found out I was pregnant. Morning sickness came on with full force.

I am sure I wasn't the only pregnant student on campus, but it sure felt like it. I certainly felt different because of my condition, but no one made me feel bad, at least not to my face.

One day between classes, I grabbed lunch with a friend. I chose a huge, thick square of lemon cake with the sweet glaze icing on top. I took a big bite of the cake and a big swig of milk and savored the taste. Seconds later, I felt a rumbling in my stomach. "Uh oh," I said, eyes wide with fear. She looked at me, confused, but there was no time to explain. I jumped up and bolted down the hallway, saw a bathroom, pushed the door open, and headed into the nearest stall. The baby had done it again. My lemon cake and milk were in the toilet.

"Are you okay?" a fellow classmate asked with concern in her voice

"Yes, I'm pregnant, and I guess what I was eating upset my stomach," I said. "I'll be alright."

I washed up and headed out the door.

I still didn't know what I wanted to do, and I now felt especially out of place. Luckily, I was able to fill my schedule with general education courses before I had to officially declare a major. This bought me valuable time as I tried to sort out my life.

While I didn't feel particularly judged at school, I felt more judgment about the pregnancy from my high school friends. I knew they were all talking about me. I had faced a lot of scrutiny because of my relationship with my boyfriend while we were in high school. He was a playboy (these days they call them fuckboys) and thought very highly of himself, which didn't sit well with many people. So being pregnant just gave folks something to talk about. Out of the blue a random friend from high school who I hadn't talked to since graduation would call to ask how I was doing, fishing for information. I knew exactly what they were calling for. I even had one friend pop me upside my head like I was a bad little kid when I told her I was pregnant. It was like they were all on the sidelines waiting for me to fail. It bothered me, but I took it all in stride and made the best of it. I would not give them the satisfaction of watching me fail.

Despite some of the negativity, there were many wonderful times during my pregnancy. At some point my mother told my great-grandmother that I was pregnant. From that day forward, every time I went to her room to see her, she'd ask, "Where's the baby?"

"She's not here yet, Mother Dear, not until May," I'd answer with a smile. I found out much later that at nineteen my great-grandmother was already married to her first husband back in Tulsa, Oklahoma, so the idea of starting a family so young wasn't out of the ordinary at all. Mother Dear was almost 100 years old in 1997, and I believe the anticipation of the pregnancy is what kept her with us. She got to spend three months with her great-great-granddaughter before she died.

My prenatal visits were also a great experience. As soon as I received the positive pregnancy test, where I once scheduled shopping trips to the Inglewood Swapmeet, I now scheduled and attended all my prenatal care visits. My doctor was an older Nigerian man who practiced in a medical office in downtown Inglewood, just a few miles south of our home. The office was in a large house, so it felt like going to a home, not some sterile medical office. It had a homey feel, I suppose because it was an actual house! The large white home sat behind a huge tree on a large lot on the corner of a mildly busy street. It was an odd sight among the clothing stores, beauty salons, and other miscellaneous businesses along the main strip. The waiting room was a living room and was always full of pregnant women and moms with their little babies. I learned a lot about my body and my growing baby during those visits. The staff were patient and answered all my questions.

Then there was my baby shower. A lot of my friends and family showed up, and we played games and ate food and caught up on what everyone was doing. It was a beautiful day and it felt good to be supported. My mother made sure to take photos of everything that was happening, only to find out later that the camera wasn't even turned on. I only have one photo of that day of me holding the remnants of my baby shower cake.

If you had told me then that my experience as a pregnant teen would be part of the path that led me to be such an advocate and teacher in public health, I would have laughed. That I would literally live and breathe public health concepts like structural racism and the social determinants of health was not something in the forefront of my mind at the time. A lot of survival mode was integrated in the next few decades of my life. Yet, looking back I know that life experiences shape us for what we can then teach and further understand. Growing up and not being confident about my body, feeling out of place in college because I was the embodiment of a timeworn stereotype of the young black teen mother, and living with the general feeling of being less than as a black woman helped me to see all the areas in society where women who looked like me are marginalized. Although these experiences were painful, I am grateful for them because they gave me the insight in my work in public health to look for the "gaps"—the places in society where the perspectives of black women were missing—and work tirelessly in my career to fill those gaps for other populations that have been overlooked.

Chapter Five

Teen Single Mom at USC

Teen motherhood could have changed my life for the worse. Many young women that get pregnant as teens don't have the resources and opportunities to continue their education and end up leaving high school, never mind making it to college. I was blessed that my mom watched Andréa so I could continue college. Dropping out of school can have a huge impact on future income, which can lead many families into poverty. Poverty is a significant determinant of health status and life expectancy. I was fortunate to have a strong support system that made it possible to stay in school, which ensured that I would be able to support my daughter. My mother literally took my baby and said, "Go to school," and I did.

I am very aware of the privilege I had. Some young mothers are from one-income, single-parent families. Grandma cannot stay home and watch the baby; she has to work! I don't know what I would have done if my mother had not been there. Child care for infants can be very expensive. If my daughter got pregnant today, I would not be able to do what my mother did for me. I am the sole income earner in my home. There is a mortgage to pay and lots of bills that I am responsible for.

To add to how much was changing in my life, several months before the birth, Andréa's father broke up with me over the phone.

"I think we should be friends…" he said.

Time stopped. How could we be "friends" when our child was on the way? I was so sad. I felt like I had already let my family down by being a teen mother, and now I was a SINGLE teen mother.

I wanted us to stay together. I struggled with my heartache, but I quickly had to accept appreciation that he would be there through the birth and after. He wasn't bailing out on the baby. He was just dumping me. I couldn't see it then, but that was the best gift ever.

One solace I had to all the unexpected changes was my due date, May 26, 1997. Spring semester would be over, which meant I could finish all my classes, take my finals, deliver my baby, and spend the entire summer with her before heading back to class in the fall. Perfect. I was fortunate to live at home with my parents still, and so I wouldn't have the pressure of work or school.

One morning that March, a familiar cramping feeling woke me from my sleep. Under normal circumstances, I'd lament that my period was starting. Except, I wasn't menstruating because I was thirty-one weeks pregnant. I jumped up and headed to my parents' room.

"Mom, something's wrong, I'm cramping," I said with fear in my voice.

She jumped up, got dressed, and in a flash, we were in the car headed to the hospital.

We arrived at Daniel Freeman Hospital around 6:00 a.m. came out of nowhere and placed me in a wheelchair. I felt strange being in that chair, like an old feeble person. I was wheeled inside to check in.

"Did you do advanced check-in?" the person behind the desk asked with a nice and calm voice despite all of the commotion

"No," I said quietly. I felt terrible, but then I realized my daughter wasn't due for two more months, so of course I hadn't checked in yet.

The next thing I knew, I was in a bland hospital room with some sort of contraption on me to measure my contractions. I wasn't savvy enough to know how to properly time them or how to manage them. I just braced for them as they came and waited for them to subside. My mother was there with me, offering her support and encouragement. I was scared.

My daughter's father arrived at some point. I was surprised to see him there.

The doctor finally walked in, washed his hands, put on his gloves, and examined me.

"This baby is coming today. You are fully dilated," he declared.

Fully dilated? What? How? It was not time for her to come. She was supposed to be born May 26! After finals and the end of the semester! I couldn't believe it, but there was nothing I could do. She was coming. I had a plan, and her coming now was not in the agenda.

Soon after hearing this news, it was delivery time.

"Who is going with her?" the doctor asked.

There was a pregnant pause. My daughter's father hesitated and stepped back, sending a clear message with his body language that he would not be there to guide me through this process. My mother stepped forward. "I'll go."

I was so relieved and grateful. My mom had been my biggest support during my pregnancy. I couldn't imagine going in there alone; her support meant everything. I don't know how women manage without a mom, aunt, or friend to help. For women who don't have friends or family nearby, finding a source of support can be challenging. Social media has become a great space to find like-minded people to share resources and lift each other up. The church can also be a place to find a strong support group.

I was wheeled down a long hallway to the delivery room. The nurses and the doctor prepared me for the grand occasion. I didn't have time to think or take in all that was happening. Life was going at lightning speed at that moment.

They broke my water, and soon after I heard the famous words from the doctor.

"I need you to push," he said calmly to me.

I was covered in sweat and everything was moving so fast. I made a short grunting sound and did a quick push, like I was doing "number two."

"No, you need to PUSH!" he said, showing how I should push the baby out. I had not been to Lamaze class, so I had NO clue what I was supposed to do. I didn't know how to do any of that "he he he" breathing. I was winging it. I had no birthing plan, and I was not prepared at all. What I did know was that the pain was unbearable. It felt like I was trying to pass a basketball through my vagina. It was easily the worst pain I had ever felt.

But after three hours of labor, it was all over. Andréa A'jane Hamilton was born. She weighed three pounds, eleven ounces, and was eight weeks early. My mother and I cried as Andréa arrived. I only heard a tiny cry from her as they rushed her to the NICU.

I spent as much time with her as I could. She was so tiny in her hospital incubator. Her head full of hair was covered with a tiny knit hat and she had all sorts of sensors on her, monitoring her vital signs. I was released from the hospital on Friday, I went to church that Easter Sunday, and I returned to school on Monday. I'm pretty sure I was supposed to spend time resting and recuperating after giving birth, but I didn't know any better and no one tried to stop me. I am a firm believer in the benefit of being "young and dumb." Sometimes being oblivious or unaware of limitations or barriers can be beneficial. Not knowing what you're not "supposed" to do gives you room to grow and stretch your horizons, an opportunity to take a chance and go with it. If I had stopped to think about the enormity of my situation, that I had just literally given birth less than a week before returning to class, I might have convinced myself to stay out of school. I would have certainly held myself back. A great example of the" young and dumb" philosophy at work occurred during a meeting with a college advisor. After I shared my difficulties with school, how I was having trouble passing my classes and settling on a major, I also shared that I was struggling with pregnancy and motherhood.

"Maybe you should take a leave of absence," he suggested with concern in his voice.

Why would he suggest I leave school? I thought to myself, certain he did not understand me at all or my experiences. After all, he was an older white man; he most certainly had never been a pregnant or parenting teen while trying to attend college. I'm sure he meant well, but his suggestion didn't resonate with me.

I thanked him for his advice and went on about my day. Why would I leave my education? I had worked really hard to get to USC, and to take a leave of absence seemed like admitting defeat, like giving up on myself. I was certain that if I took a leave of absence, finding my way back to finish my degree would be hard. Besides, my pregnancy wasn't some tragedy that was plopped in front of me unknowingly. Obviously having a baby is a process that I was fully invested in. Not planned, but certainly no accident. There would be no leave of absence for me. I wished he would have asked me what I needed help with and offered me resources to help me navigate school as a new mom.

Andréa stayed in the NICU for three weeks. It was terrible to see her there in the incubator. Although it was a very difficult time, there were many advantages. Since I had not taken Lamaze or parenting class during my pregnancy, the extra time in the hospital allowed me to get lessons from the nurses on how to take care of her. I was so grateful for the time I had with those nurses. They helped me learn the most important fundamentals in caring for my daughter. I learned how to bathe her, how to change her diaper, how to feed her, and the importance of skin to skin contact for her growth and development. The nurses were so knowledgeable, helpful, and patient. The other advantage to an otherwise bad situation was the extra time we got at home to prepare for her arrival.

As helpful as the nurses were, there was one thing that I couldn't quite figure out as a new mother. I tried to breastfeed exclusively when Andréa was born but didn't have enough information or support to remain consistent. I was offered the use of an electric breast pump just once to help me pump breastmilk. I didn't get to speak with a lactation consultant or anyone who could help me figure out how to breastfeed consistently. When I got out of the hospital, I was given samples of formula, which sends the wrong message about breastfeeding to a new mom. As a result, I didn't have enough milk to send to the hospital, and they began giving her formula. I would learn later in my public health career that African American moms breastfeed at rates much lower than mothers of other races. This is due to several factors including lack of breastfeeding support and resources. I also learned that hospitals can play an integral part in determining the success of breastfeeding moms by becoming "baby friendly": allowing mom and baby to room together twenty-four hours a day, helping mom start breastfeeding within one hour after birth, not offering baby formula or pacifiers, showing mom how to breastfeed, and offering breastfeeding support groups. Unfortunately, none of these resources and practices were available in the hospital where I delivered my daughter. In fact, the first hospital in the state to go baby friendly is over 150 miles away from my home and received the designation a year after Andréa was born. Today there are ten baby friendly hospitals within ten miles of my home, a huge improvement from twenty years ago. The implications of delivering in a hospital that is not baby friendly were very real for me. I didn't receive adequate breastfeeding support in the hospital or after delivery. By the time I brought her home three weeks after delivery I was primarily bottle feeding her. I could have worked to bring my supply back up, but there were other barriers to contend with. I returned to school and work soon after she was born and couldn't quite figure out how to manage it all. Putting her on the bottle seemed like my only option at the time.

Once the decision was made to move to formula feeding, I went to the local grocery store near my obstetrician's office to pick up a few cans. I made my way to the aisle with all the baby items and found the formula

"Twenty dollars!" I muttered to myself after looking at the price on the can. "I can't afford this!"

I was stuck. I couldn't breastfeed effectively, and the price of formula was too expensive. I didn't want to go on welfare. My daughter's father was helping, but he didn't have a lot of money either, and I certainly didn't want to burden my parents with my expenses. This was my child, not theirs. Someone at work mentioned WIC (a federally funded supplemental nutrition program for women, infants, and children), and I was resistant to the idea until I was told it was not welfare or food stamps. I signed up for the program and began receiving vouchers for formula and other food items for my growing baby until she was almost five years old. I appreciated the assistance with formula during infancy and food pantry staples as she got older. I was able to pick up cheese, juice, cereal, milk, and other items for her at no cost but no fresh fruits and vegetables with the vouchers. Instead the options were fruit juice, which was full of sugar. No alternatives were available. A decade later, the WIC program introduced new guidelines for some of the food items they provided to families. Instead of milk, recipients could choose yogurt, soy milk, or tofu and replace bread with tortillas, pasta, or brown rice. The change had been thirty years in the making according to the presenters. Unfortunately, it was a decade too late for my daughter to benefit.

African Americans have the highest rates of infant mortality in the United States. More black babies die before their first birthday than any other group of infants. What's more disturbing is that factors that protect the health of other infants do not provide the same level of protection for black babies. For example, higher education levels of mothers typically protect babies from illness or death. For black women, this is not the case. Black women with college degrees have similar birth outcomes as white women with high school diplomas. In other words, their educational status does not offer any protection against infant mortality. Although my daughter did not die, my college education did not protect her from being born too soon. Prematurity is a leading cause of infant mortality among black women. The constant stress of structural racism causes the bodies of black women to age prematurely and poor health. Although the term "black don't crack" is often used to describe black women's amazing ability to seemingly age backwards, the real story is that we are aging prematurely on the inside, where the most damage is being done.

There was so much to learn as a new mom, and I didn't pretend to have all the answers. As much as I was learning and adjusting to my new role, her father also was quickly adapting to his role. Stress contributes to a lot of illness in this country, and divorce, shared custody, and single parenting is an area where we can get very run-down and burdened by our emotions and the weight of handling it all. Although we did not stay together, he was actively engaged in her upbringing as was the rest of his family. Therefore, custody and visitation during those early years were a continual negotiation. Soon after she was born, we went to court to determine custody and visitation issues. I would miss class to visit Levitt and Quinn, the low-income family law center, to get help completing legal documents or to go to court. I was awarded full physical custody and we shared joint legal custody. Her dad had regular visitation. Those early days of visitation were very hard. The visits were very short, only a couple of hours; and since she was still a baby, many of the visitations were at my home or close to home. He didn't feel welcome or comfortable visiting his daughter in my home because there was a lot of anger and ego and hurt on both sides of the family. We did our best to keep Andréa out of it, but we weren't always successful. Tensions often ran high.

Once when Andréa was about three years old, we got into an argument about her hair. Yes, her hair. I had sent her with her dad with one hair style and she came back with a different hair style. In hindsight, it wasn't really anything to be upset about, but I was pissed off about it. She was MY daughter. Why was someone else (probably some girl he was seeing) touching her hair? All I know is during the argument he called me stupid or dumb, which is a trigger word for me, and I was done. I threw my USC diploma at him, Andréa got mad at me, and my dad had to calm everybody down. Fun times indeed.

I had friends to talk to, but no one really understood what I was going through. There wasn't a place that I was aware of in my community that I could go and talk with other young women about motherhood and co-parenting and get support and encouragement. Many women I knew just bottled up their feelings and went about their lives or took their pain and frustration out on those closest to them. Both options can be very detrimental to mental and physical health.

As my daughter got older, the visits with her dad were extended. Eventually her dad would keep her for a week and bring her back home and leave her with me for a week. When he requested this change in visitation, I was a ball of emotion. Spending more time with her father would develop their bond, but who would help Andréa with her homework? My brain could not comprehend that her dad would obviously take care of it. I was so used to managing almost every aspect of her life that it was hard to consider that her dad, however capable he was, could take care of it. I also worried about what my parents would say.

Although I was living on my own, their opinion still meant a lot to me. After thinking about it for a while, I eventually relented and allowed the new schedule. At first it was really hard to let her go for so long, but over time I came to appreciate the time I had to myself. I was able to really expand who I was beyond my role as Andréa's mother. It allowed me to spend time resting or explore aspects of my own adult life free from just "mom." Every mom needs the time to focus on their own growth and development. That very first week was very hard for me. I was used to having Andréa around and making sure she was at school on time, got her work done, and went to bed at a reasonable hour. Of course, her father was capable of managing her needs. It wasn't that I didn't trust that he would do a good job. I had to adjust to the shift. I very quickly came to appreciate the extra time spent in bed catching a few more minutes of sleep and the time and gas saved from having to take her to school. I was able to dedicate time to self-care, to exploring the things that made me who I am. In turn, I was a better mother because I was rested and recharged.

While my life has been blessed with motherhood, my story is a cautionary tale. Young women, seriously vet the person you wish to have children with because you will be tied to them for life (or at least until the child is eighteen years old). The question should not be, "Is he cute?" but rather "Is he stable, mentally, spiritually, and economically?" A mature approach to having a child is discussing whether there are shared views on parenting style, discipline, and overall life goals. My daughter's father and I were no longer together, and as much as it hurt me at the time, it didn't take very long to realize that it was for the best. We were not compatible as partners but had to work together for Andréa. Time does heal. We eventually figured out a way to communicate and work together while causing the least amount of stress and strife. Minimizing stress is beneficial to all parties involved, especially young children who should not have to absorb any of the stress caused by family conflict. I couldn't wait until she turned eighteen, though, because I knew I would no longer have reason to co-parent with him. She could maintain a relationship with her father on her own.

And don't get me wrong, from the start as a teen mom at USC there were many moments of happiness. I would sometimes dress Andréa in a cute outfit complete with her white, soft-soled walking shoes with little bells on the shoestrings, comb her hair into little ponytails with colorful barrettes, and take her with me to school. I was exposing her to higher education and setting her on a positive trajectory. Once there I'd place her in her navy blue and white stroller with hearts all over it and we'd walk across campus to class. The students loved her! She was a quiet baby and she'd sit there in class, watching me and everyone else, kicking her feet around which caused it to sound like Christmas time in there with all the noise from the bells. When I didn't bring her, the students would ask me where she was. I felt happy knowing they liked having her, and me, around.

Bringing her to school also exposed how unfriendly the campus was to people who needed assistance getting around. I had to look for wheelchair ramps and elevators on campus and sometimes it was very hard to find them when needed. I took her with me once to purchase my textbooks for the coming semester. The campus was alive and full of excited students ready to start school. It was a beautiful and warm August day when we got to the front of the campus bookstore. I walked right to the front of the building and came to an abrupt stop, confused about what to do next. Under normal circumstances I'd walk up the two flights of stairs that were in front of the building and walk right into the bookstore without thinking twice. Somehow, I had forgotten the stairs were there and was perplexed about how I would get myself and Andréa into the bookstore. Someone kindly helped me lift the stroller up the stairs and we headed inside only to find that we had to walk all the way to the back of the building to a tiny elevator that took us upstairs to the textbooks. I wondered how people who use wheelchairs felt being relegated to the back of buildings to find ramps and elevators. The experience was dehumanizing and frustrating, like we didn't belong or were an afterthought. Andréa and I just pushed forward and got it done.

I firmly believe being a teen mom propelled me further in the RIGHT direction more than anything else. I was a good kid anyway, and I was going to finish college ANYWAY, but it was an opportunity for life to take a turn for the worse, and it didn't. Motherhood was about thinking ahead and considering the life of someone else that depended on me for everything. Most importantly, being a mother was a lesson in navigating around roadblocks that would serve me well later in life.

Chapter Six

Clarity in My Public Health Profession

had vacillated on declaring a major for a few semesters, but by my twentieth birthday and sophomore year, my path in school got much clearer. I discovered that I wanted to help people get access to medical care by opening a health clinic for low-income residents. It was a lofty goal, and I had no idea how I would achieve it. I didn't even know what major I needed to declare to set me on this path. I didn't know the first step in attempting to open a health care facility. My thoughts about this hadn't been fully fleshed out, and my limited view of health care left me a bit confused about how I could make a difference. Yet I had a hunch that health care was my path.

I first had to decide what part of the vast health care system at which to direct my focus. I had already figured out that direct patient care wasn't for me when I did poorly in my science classes and couldn't get beyond the excitement of skinning a dead cat in anatomy class to actually focus and learn the body parts like I was supposed to. I thought I had to be a doctor or nurse or pharmacist to help people improve their health. I mustered the courage to ask for help and received important guidance from a black woman on faculty at the university. She was part of the Center for Black Cultural and Student Affairs, an important resource for black students on campus. I told her that I wanted to open a health clinic for low-income residents. I had just gone through a very frustrating time trying to work through the health care system for Andréa, and I wanted to make sure others didn't have such a hard time.

"You know you don't have to be a doctor to open a health clinic. You can get a degree in health policy or health administration," she said

I was relieved! Now I had a sense of direction and purpose.

I also had a "genetic" predisposition to helping people. My grandfather, my mom, and my aunt all worked in helping professions and have done great work over the years helping people in one way or another. I felt the same responsibility to help others, just as they had done.

I declared my undergraduate degree in Public Policy and Management focused on Health Care Policy. I wasn't 100% sure about what I would do with the degree but at least the pressure was off regarding what I would major in. I enrolled in classes for my major and got to work. I took classes with titles like "Public Organizations and Management," "Introduction to Health Care Systems," and "Simulated Policymaking in Urban Systems: Theory and Practice." That last class was very hard for me, but it was the most realistic. We learned all the theory about policymaking, and at some point, we were assigned roles in a fictional city government and put to work with a simulator that would spit out a report about the happenings in the city that was formatted like a newspaper. Each week we'd read the headlines based on our previous interactions and work with each other in real time regarding the issues that came up to get the needs of the city met. I was a leader of a community-based organization in the class and had to try to prevent a highway or some other sort of imposition from happening to the community. I was still very quiet as a student, so I didn't quite master the art of advocating for the pretend residents, but it was an eye-opening experience!

Although there were quite a few black students and employees at

USC, I only had one black professor during my undergraduate career. She taught one of the undergrad Public Policy and Management classes.

One day she asked the class, "What do you think of when you hear the term 'healthy family'?" The usual occurred whenever a professor asked the classroom a question: dead silence. Eventually a few brave souls made a guess: "A two parent household" was put forth as a suggestion.

Isn't she talking about the health insurance program for low-income people? I thought to myself. I didn't want to be wrong, so I didn't say anything.

Sure enough, she was talking about the health insurance program available for low-income residents. I had firsthand personal experience with public insurance programs when the three-week stay in the NICU for Andréa, along with her delivery, cost forty thousand dollars. My parents' insurance paid for all my prenatal care, so we assumed they would cover my daughter's hospital stay. They did not as they determined that she had a pre-existing condition because she was born premature. This was thirteen years before the passage of the Patient Protection and Affordable Care Act, which offers insurance protections to people with pre-existing conditions. I had to apply for Medi-Cal to get her hospital bill paid and also had to navigate the very complex and unfriendly process of getting her adequate health coverage. Lots of paperwork and annual recertifications made it a nightmare to keep coverage. In other words, she was talking about people like me that were Medi-Cal eligible. Imagine if in class there had been an opportunity for us to get to know each other. The conversation about Healthy Families would have been quite robust and enriching. We could have talked about the financial burden that is lifted from families when their children have access to health care and are not relegated to emergency room visits, which are much more costly than a visit with a primary care physician. My classmates, who didn't look like me or have a similar life experience, would have had firsthand insight into what it means to have access to resources such as Healthy Families. Although it can be difficult to do, students who find themselves in a situation such as this one should try to speak up about it, either in class or to their professor. Sharing experiences such as the one I had helps students understand the varied experiences of their classmates and hopefully provides much-needed nuance to the often abstract and theoretical concepts taught in class.

Ironically, Dr. Lavonna Blair Lewis and I were reacquainted many years later in our work to improve the health of South Central Los Angeles residents. I have lectured or sat on panels for her class and have provided support in any way possible. Recently I discovered that she is a neighbor as well. I am able to give back to a school that I once felt so apart from and provide that unique perspective to students who may not have ever visited the inner city or talked candidly about race, class, power, and privilege in regards to public health. What I didn't have the courage to speak up about as a student. There's no question that Los Angeles County is rich with history and very diverse, but underneath the façade of glamour and liberalness lies a dirty secret. Despite this diversity, there are very large differences in the health status of the folks that live here.

What I first learned as a Public Policy and Management major was that health care is an important part of the country's infrastructure. The goal is to ensure access to affordable and quality health care for everyone. Health care focuses on the treatment or cure of an individual who is already sick, offering them medication, surgery, or some other option to treat or cure their condition. I would find out very soon that public health, the field I would ultimately choose to work in, is a much broader discipline. The quote "an ounce of prevention is worth a pound of cure" is basically a public health concept. Public health finds ways to keep people from getting sick in the first place. This can mean promoting concepts as simple as handwashing to prevent colds and flu and as complex as eliminating structural racism to improve birth outcomes for black babies.

Still needing a job to support myself and Andréa, I moved from my food service job on campus to a student worker position at the local health department. I was so excited when I finally scored an interview. I put on my best outfit and went to meet Rose Wang, one of the managers of a program at the department. The office was in an old building just south of downtown Los Angeles, steps away from the 110 freeway. The first floor housed County social services such as food stamps and GR (or general relief, also known as welfare). The building was terribly outdated. The floors were cracked and old, and the walls were a shade of sickly yellow. Once I passed security, to my surprise, the elevator was staffed! A lady took people from floor to floor. The building was so old that the elevator had to be operated by hand. She was an eccentric lady who wore lots of makeup and butterflies in her hair. She was sweet and struck up conversation with everyone as she took people from floor to floor. Many years later they finally replaced that old elevator but during the time I was there, "butterfly lady" took us from floor to floor.

I ended up not getting the job. Years later Rose told me I was too vibrant and full of life to be placed in the position she had to offer. Instead, she referred me to a colleague down that hall who was also hiring. What happened next would set me on a path that was life changing to my career. She sent me to talk to Diane Brown. Diane was the lead for the Health Education Unit at the Sexually Transmitted Disease Program. Yes, STDs!

She needed a student worker to support the work of the health educators as they did the noble and often difficult work of educating the many diverse populations of the county of Los Angeles on the dangers of STDs, providing resources for treatment and offering condoms. I was intrigued by the work (especially considering my fear of buying condoms as a teen) and luckily was offered the job soon afterwards.

The work was exciting. The staff at the STD Program focused on prevention among populations of people. The classes I took in college focused on public policy and health care administration, which mainly focuses on medical care and treatment after someone is sick. The idea of prevention made perfect sense to me, and the work I was doing was amazing. I was sold on the concept of public health.

I accompanied the health educators to talk about STDs to all kinds of community groups. I helped put together presentations on various STDs. I showed students in schools how to properly put on condoms (using a banana or a dildo). I consulted on set for an STD campaign commercial. For example, they totally had the name of the boyfriend wrong for the black girl so I helped them pick a better name that would resonate with the people they were hoping would watch the commercial. The most interesting part of the job was answering the STD hotline. The stigma attached to sexual health can be stifling, and dangerous! People would call and describe their symptoms hoping that I could diagnose them over the phone because they were so afraid to go to a clinic. There was the one guy that, without fail, called at least once a month to ask how to put a condom on. The kicker was that at some point during the conversation he'd say, "I can't seem to figure out how to put it on. In fact, I'm trying to put it on right now while I'm talking to you and I'm having so much trouble." He'd get us every time! I guess we were his free monthly sex call.

Another time I got a call from a woman asking about her recent STD diagnosis. She told me that her boyfriend told her that she must have gotten the disease from a toilet seat. I told her that wasn't true and that was not how sexually transmitted diseases were passed from one person to another. I could tell she was upset, but it was my responsibility to give her accurate information. We got off the phone. Minutes later the phone rang again. It was the same lady and this time she had her boyfriend on the phone. It was VERY uncomfortable to be in the middle of that conversation. I imagined the difficult position the woman was in: she was probably embarrassed and angry that this had happened to her, she had to consider that her partner was cheating on her, and she probably still had feelings for him as well. It's a tough spot to be in. I provided as much information as I could through all the arguing and eventually ended the call.

I truly enjoyed my time at the STD Program. I met so many wonderful professionals that I am still close to now. They have become colleagues and friends. It was there that my love of public health began. It was also there that I decided to further my education.

I would learn much later as I entered public health as my field of career interest that these issues are important public health issues that lead to high rates of teen pregnancy and STD infection since the same activity that causes pregnancy can also cause disease.

The good news is that overall, teen pregnancy rates are much lower now than they were when I was growing up. However, the rates of sexually transmitted disease continue to rise, especially among young folks. The general public tends to think it has to do with a lack of education about sexual and reproductive health. It's definitely part of the problem! I've given many presentations on STDs to young folks in my professional career and the questions about anatomy are mind blowing. Our young people don't always get the most accurate information about their bodies and resort to coming to their own conclusions or listening to friends who also don't have the right information.

Another concern is the interesting contradiction about sex in our society. We really, really, really like sex. We like to talk about it, watch it on TV, sing about it, rap about it, and do it. But we really don't like to talk about safe sex, and we don't like to talk about what happens when unsafe sex happens. We love the feeling but don't necessarily want to put much thought into being responsible with sexual relations.

Stigma and shame regarding sex, STDs, and teen pregnancy are barriers to healthy sexual lives, which can have long-lasting impacts. If teens aren't given proper information about their bodies and how to effectively prevent themselves from sexually transmitted disease and pregnancy, they may end up in a situation that is not so easy to get out of. For example, teen pregnancy not only impacts the young mother's potential for economic stability because she may have to leave or delay her education, but the young father may have to leave school to work, which decreases his likelihood of higher wages for his new family, which could leave his children impoverished.

Some STDs can cause infertility, so a wrong choice in high school can impact a person's decision to have a family at age thirty. Young folks are often ashamed to seek help regarding symptoms they may be having, which makes them fearful of showing up at a clinic for regular testing. The stereotype is that only nasty or promiscuous people have lots of sex and therefore end up with disease or pregnancy. What people don't realize is that sexual networks in a community have much more to do with disease than anything else. If a person is picking sex partners in a community with high rates of disease, the person will be more likely to encounter disease. It's a pure numbers game and doesn't really have anything to do with how promiscuous a person is. A person can have many sex partners in a community with low rates of disease and not get an STD because the odds are lower. They're not safer or purer, they're just luckier. It only takes one interaction with one infected partner to get an STD. The same is true with pregnancy. It just takes one interaction without a condom to get someone pregnant.

A year after I started at the STD Program, I successfully completed my undergraduate program. It took me four and a half years. Taking an extra semester to finish was a small price to pay considering I completed my entire college experience as a single mother. Although I could have participated in commencement exercises in summer 2000 with the rest of my class, I decided to walk across the stage in May 2001 when all my classes were complete, and my degree was conferred. Black graduation, the ceremony that I was most excited to participate in, was at Bovard Auditorium in the center of campus. All the black students on campus that were graduating that year were lined up outside Bovard. We looked so collegiate in our black caps and gowns and our graduation stoles made with kente cloth. It was so ironic to be standing in the same spot I was in eight years earlier dressed in all white graduating from junior high school. It was a full circle moment. As we waited in line to walk into the building, I chatted it up with students I had met during my studies. The mood was jubilant. Everyone was excited. As we entered the building, there were cheers from the crowd. The auditorium was filled with friends, family, siblings, and loved ones who had come to see their graduate walk across the stage. We were the representation of the fulfillment of a dream, an investment in the future, and these families were there to witness it all. When the emcee called my name, I walked across the stage with a smile on my face. I was so proud of myself. I had completed my goal, and now it was time to celebrate.

At the end of the ceremony, I walked out with all the other graduates and looked for my family. There were hundreds of people there waiting to meet up with their graduates. I don't know how, but I immediately found my family and began to cry. The realization that it was all over finally hit me. I had done it! Andréa, a preschooler at the time, took one look at me and started crying too! I don't know if she was overwhelmed by the noise, or if she was in tune with my emotions at the moment, but I picked her up and my family and I headed home.

Although I loved my job at the STD Program, I couldn't stay forever. Part of the requirement of the student professional worker position was that I had to be a student. I was able to fly under the radar for a little while, but after my graduation in 2001, I had to start looking for a job. I didn't have to go far to find it. My first "real" job was at the Head Start program run by USC. Head Start is a federally funded program that provides preschool to low-income children three to five years old as well as resources and support services to families. In essence, giving children a "head start" in their growth and development and preparing them for kindergarten. As I child I attended a Head Start program at my grandmother's church, so I was a direct beneficiary of the program. At USC Head Start I was the Health Services Coordinator, ensuring that all of the preschoolers at the three locations run by the program had their immunizations and all the health resources they needed. I loved working with the families and the amazing service providers, such as Jules Stein/UCLA Mobile Eye Clinic and John Tracy Clinic, who gave amazing health resources to the students. My coworkers were amazing as well and came from many different backgrounds. My time at Head Start brought to light the association between health and wealth, one of the main public health issues in our society. Many of the children and their families had black and Latino mothers who were poor and often weren't very healthy. I often saw mothers holding babies with mouths full of either silver fillings or missing or rotten teeth, victims of baby bottle tooth decay. The communities that the families lived in lacked adequate resources and the homes the families lived in were often substandard.

Seeing the families in the program reminded me that poverty is the single greatest indicator of health status in the world. Poor people have worse health than those who are affluent. Part of the issue is affordability. People with greater incomes can afford better health care, but there is more to the story. Lower incomes are associated with lower sense of control of destiny and higher stress levels. It's not just about not being able to afford health care; it's about poor people's bodies literally being worn down due to the enormous amount of stress they encounter by just trying get by.

Re-enter the social determinants of health. Educational attainment, housing, and employment. Think about it: if the education system in a community is poor, not only will the community suffer due to poor economic outcomes, they will also have poor health outcomes due to inability to acquire gainful employment, lack of adequate health education courses that teach positive health behaviors, and lack of social support. I was literally seeing these concepts in real time, right in front of me, and it was very real and very raw. The families were doing the best they could, but they could not get up from the crushing weight of poverty, racism, low-quality or nonexistent jobs, and poor housing that was suffocating the entire community. Programs like Head Start were doing the best they could to help, but the problem was so large and woven into the systems and institutions of the community that it seemed that nothing could fix it. I could not unsee what I was seeing, and I had more questions than answers.

My desire to expand my education in public health was piqued at Head Start. I thought back to my colleagues at the STD Program. The health educators that I worked with had Master of Public Health degrees and were trained to assess public health issues, develop programs and interventions to solve them, and then evaluate those programs to see if they worked. They also were able to take complicated health information and translate it into plain language to ensure residents understood the information and could act on it. They had an amazing arsenal of knowledge and were creating widespread change. I knew getting a master's degree and extending my education beyond an undergraduate degree would give me even more tools and concepts to apply to my work in public health, as well as my many teaching positions over the last decade. A graduate education is also important economically.

While employed at the Head Start program, I kept coming back to the realization that health care and resources were not enough to improve the health of the families that participated in the program. The issues were simply too big. I needed to be part of the solution at the population level and work to change our societal systems and institutions, which is where change ultimately occurs. In order to do that I needed the skillset that the health educators at my old job had. I looked into the Master of Public Health Program at USC. As a USC employee, I qualified for tuition reduction, which would be tremendously helpful in keeping my student debt low. It was a perfect arrangement.

When I worked at the STD Program, I became friends with one of my earliest mentors in the Department, Dr. Lisa Smith. Dr. Smith is an epidemiologist and professor at UCLA. She never hesitated to share with me her knowledge and perspective. At the time, she worked with all the data at the STD Program. On one occasion I was in her cubicle and we were having a conversation about my future.

"Okay, Pookie," (she called everyone Pookie), "are you going to go to graduate school? It's only two years and your salary will double." She wanted me to advance my career and gain economic security for myself and my daughter.

I lamented about the additional time in school, but she was ready for my pushback.

"The time will pass anyway, Pookie. You might as well spend it in school," she said, looking at me with a straight face. Of course, she was right!

So I took the leap.

I spent many months studying for the GRE exam and preparing my personal statement. I pushed back those familiar feelings of not being good enough as I grew frustrated and emotional after getting GRE test questions wrong or rewriting my personal statement for the millionth time. I was so certain that this was what I wanted to do that the feelings of inadequacy were not enough to stop me. After a nerve-wracking GRE exam where I cried in the parking lot after seeing my barely passing score, I turned in my application and waited. I was accepted into the program and began graduate school in 2003. Andréa was in the first grade, which allowed me to work full-time and go to school full-time while she was in class. My parents and her father once again stepped up and supported my ambition by picking up Andréa from school while I had class and helping wherever needed.

I loved graduate school and was adapting the important concepts that I learned in class to my work at the Head Start program. The arrangement was perfect. School complimented work and vice versa, which gave me an advantage for future job prospects because I was actively working in the field where I was obtaining my graduate school degree. Many of my classmates had gone straight to graduate school from undergrad and had very little work experience. I was already a working professional. I had firsthand experience working with some of the populations that were used as examples in class. I also had experience with assessment, program planning, and evaluation that many of my classmates were being exposed to for the first time. Working and going to school at the same time also forced me to be laser focused and disciplined. I didn't have the luxury of additional time to waste.

Halfway through my graduate school education, I was forced to leave my job at the Head Start program. It was devastating to me because I would be losing my tuition benefit, but I had to go. Poor management and office politics left me no other option. I loved the work that I was doing, but for some reason the administration was not happy with me. I found out that I was slated to be fired. Leaving graduate school was not an option, so I continued my studies and relied on my old connections at the County STD Program to find employment. It was a difficult time because I had to learn to stand up for myself, look for another job, and continue my education, but I handled it all with confidence and grace. I re-entered County service in 2004 while juggling a full course load and graduated from the MPH program in 2005. I am grateful to the women at my job who supervised me during that time. They allowed me to work a flexible schedule so that I could continue my studies.

My experiences with undergrad and grad school, along with my work experience, brought home the important difference between being book smart and being street smart and that being both is optimal. It's fine to educate ourselves to be leaders in the field, but if we don't understand the perspective of those needing help, we are missing a big piece of the puzzle. If we know exactly what the scope of the issue is, then we can view any strategies or programs aimed at making communities healthier through the lens of those that are impacted.

Coming to this understanding has a lot to do with my commitment to academia and to teaching and mentoring college students. I am well aware of the impact of the teachers and mentors that helped me through school, and I can help young people in the same way for generations to come. The leaders of tomorrow will need to know now, more than ever, the subtleties and nuances of public health leadership, and it has much more to do with community, connections, and relationships than a simple textbook.

Kinship in the County Office

I n 2006, at twenty-eight years old, I got my first promotion as the only health educator in the South Los Angeles Field Office, providing public health services and programs to both West and South Los Angeles. There are four of these field offices across the county, each one providing services to approximately two million people. I had just moved out of my parents' home with my nine-year-old daughter and was looking forward to this major career move with excitement and anticipation. I would be working at Hubert H. Humphrey Comprehensive Health Center, a huge county facility on Slauson Avenue and Main Street in South Central LA. This position was my first "real" public health job after graduate school, and a few years after working at the County STD Program as a student worker, which I almost didn't get because I was at the very bottom of the hiring list. I had made quite a leap in a few short years. I was grateful for the opportunity and happy for the increased income and stability.

Working in the South LA office put me right in the center of my community on a daily basis, but I also served West LA, home to many of the wealthiest areas of Los Angeles County. I had traversed between South LA and parts of West LA growing up, but never farther West than Culver City (which had the only shopping mall in the area until South Central LA got its first mall in 1990). So I understood the economic divide from a distance and in theory. Westside cities and communities such as Malibu, Santa Monica, Brentwood, Pacific Palisades and Calabasas were distant in place and culture to me in childhood. They might as well have been foreign countries. As I came into young adulthood, the "foreign-ness" of those communities continued to create a level of discomfort for me. Barely anyone in those places looked like me, and there was an unspoken message that rang loud and clear in my ears: "This isn't your neighborhood. You don't belong here." Those communities have a wealth of resources and not very many low-income areas. Residents enjoy a high standard of living, and their health status reflects the affluence of the population. Life expectancy among West LA residents is on the higher side of the spectrum, and disease rates, for the most part, are low compared to the rest of LA County. The differences between South LA and West LA are stark, like night and day. The issues and concerns of the two areas almost never intersect, until one day in 2009 when one horrible incident shook both communities.

A young black woman named Mitrice Richardson was arrested at a Malibu restaurant after a disturbance brought on by an alleged nervous breakdown. What should have been a routine detainment turned into tragedy. Mitrice was released from custody in the middle of the night without a phone or any other means of contacting her family. A huge search for her commenced, but she was not found until a year later, when her mummified remains were found in the mountains of Malibu Canyon. The case angered me. I knew that if Mitrice was white, she would not have been let out of custody at such a late hour to fend for herself. To this day, whenever I drive to Malibu, an overwhelming feeling of dread and sadness washes over me as I reflect on what happened to Mitrice, whose death has not yet been solved. Those feelings about Mitrice are always layered over a much broader tragedy, the disparity in resources and opportunity that keep people in my community struggling to get by from one day to the next while residents in Malibu live comfortably. Disparities in resources for employment, housing, health care access, and education starve disadvantaged communities, causing residents to get stuck in a never-ending cycle of poverty, which is a key factor in poor health.

Driving up Pacific Coast Highway, I see expensive luxury cars, beautiful large homes, and an overabundance of grocery stores, parks, and open space. The last time I was in Malibu I counted one marijuana dispensary and maybe two or three liquor stores. My South Central neighborhood has few grocery stores, more liquor stores and marijuana dispensaries than I can count, people living in their cars or on the street, and crumbling infrastructure at every turn. It's unfair that our society has created systems that make such huge disparities in wealth and opportunity possible. I once read a powerful quote about creating an anti-racist society: "don't feel guilty, feel responsible." It is not the fault of the average Malibu resident that my community suffers, and they should not feel guilty for what they have acquired, but it is everyone's responsibility to push for more equitable distribution of wealth and opportunity for all.

In my position as health educator, for the next decade my job would be to serve the public health of both these communities without bias and with a wealth of empathy. There have been many tragedies of varying degrees in both communities during my career, from young community members losing their lives to gang violence, to residents killed just trying to get from one place to another, and although they were all sad and disheartening, I continued to show up to work every day to do my part to improve the health of residents.

What carried me on a day-to-day basis were the other black professional women that I worked with who stood by me and guided me on my professional journey. The women I met in those early days at the County were as passionate as I was about public health. They kept pushing me to educate myself and others and to volunteer my time and talents to improve the health of communities. The power of connection and kinship among black women must be emphasized, especially when you are in a work environment devoid of diversity because being a double minority brings its own set of challenges. Black people, especially black women, are often asked to speak on behalf of the entire black race, or we find ourselves having to fight to ensure the black perspective is included in any decisions being made. It can be disheartening to be the only black woman or one of few black women in spaces where important decisions are being made about poor people or those that are impacted by disease and disability, who are often black people. The work can be exhausting, overwhelming, and discouraging. Thoughtful feedback, insight, support, gentle correction, and encouragement from those women who cared and had already experienced what I was going through was extremely valuable in my growth and development.

Our relationships seamlessly transitioned from coworkers to friends to family. The transition was so complete that it happened like magic. The bonds I developed with these women over the years would continue to shape me both professionally and personally in ways that I could never imagine. I was stretched, molded, and pushed further and further towards possibilities that I had never considered or even imagined. The idea of black women developing and maintaining friendships with other black women seems to fly in the face of the prevailing stereotype that, especially in professional settings, we don't get along. Assumptions are made that we are always in competition with each other and seeking opportunities to bring each other down. We see this play out so often on reality television shows or videos shared on social media that it becomes fact in the minds of many people, even among black women. This stereotype is simply not true. Many of the black women that I call my friends share the same desire to improve the community and are lucky to work in professions that allow them to do so every day. Many of them are also mothers, some single, some married, all wanting what's best for their children and families. We all share a commitment to uplifting black people, specifically black women, and have a deep desire to see lasting change in South Central, where most of us live or have family ties. We also happen really like each other and enjoy each other's company. There is no jealousy or negative talk, just genuine respect and admiration.

There were two African American women I met right away in those early days that had an impact on me immediately. The first was my supervisor, Martina, a petite midwestern woman with beautiful, long, golden-brown locks tinged with gray, and one of her high-level nursing staff, Dee, also with beautiful locs and a friendly disposition. Up to that point, I had never seen black women at their age living such active and vibrant lives. The black women I had seen in their age range were often sick, overweight, and inactive. Martina and Dee were the complete opposite. They took to me almost immediately, made sure I learned everything I could about the workplace, and provided me with valuable advice on how to be a valuable member of the team and have a successful career at the County.

Also, in my role as health educator I worked side by side with public health nurses. I have always respected the nursing profession, especially the nurses that took the time to teach me everything they knew while Andréa was in the hospital shortly after her birth, but up until then I had only been exposed to nurses who worked in hospitals or convalescent homes. The public health nurses I knew worked in the community and offered education, case management, and resources to patients who had communicable disease. Most of the nurses in my workplace were black women and were products of the community where they served. Many of them worked with me on important public health programs that focused on nutrition, preparing for emergencies, sexually transmitted disease prevention, and teen pregnancy prevention. They forever changed my perception of nursing because they were passionate about their profession, cared about the community they served, and maintained a level of professionalism that was inspiring and motivating. One of those nurses, Jameelah Harris, became my first work officemate when I showed up to the South LA office all those years ago. She was slender, tall, easy to get along with, and had gone to nursing school at USC. We hit it off immediately. It was hard not to; we literally sat about four feet from each other in a tiny cramped office on the second floor at Hubert Humphrey for many years. Through job changes, relationship changes, motherhood, adjunct professorship, a doctoral program, and everything else you can imagine, Jameelah and her daughter are now considered a part of my family.

The same is true for a few others who have laughed and cried with me through all of life's twists and turns. Deanna Bressler Montgomery has worked in South LA for over twenty years as a public health nurse. Her love for the job is evident in the programs she creates, from community baby showers for teen moms at the local high school to education summits focused on preparing middle and high school students for college in communities where high school graduation rates are low. She's always the first one to volunteer to help or offer a suggestion to improve services at work. Felicia Wilson was the sweetest person I knew in the office. She offered the best advice and was non-judgmental. I was inspired by the way she approached life, with enthusiasm and wonder. She traveled a lot and saw the world, often by herself, something that wasn't on my mind at the time, but which I found to be very exciting. She passed away quite suddenly from an aggressive form of cancer at the age of fifty-two, but the way she lived her life inspired me to travel internationally and spend my time wisely. I will never forget the sound of her voice, her laugh, and all the wonderful advice she gave me about life. I do not take my professional relationships for granted and realize how lucky I am to work in an environment where people have looked out for me, have nurtured me, and have pushed me to do more. Not everyone has the same opportunities in the workforce.

After Martina retired, I gained a new supervisor, a physician named Jan King. She came to the office after a series of prospects turned down offers for the position. I suppose they were intimidated by all of the public health issues and concerns in South LA, so they all ultimately backed out. Dr. King arrived with an air of assertiveness and decisiveness, which wasn't very well received by staff who were used to Martina's mothering spirit. One of the first actions Dr. King took when she started was to meet with the hundred or so staff in the office one by one to hear what they did and what they liked and didn't like about their job. The staff was curious and a bit apprehensive about her, but I wasn't. I looked forward to my one-on-one meeting to share the work I was doing and offer information about the staff, the body of work, and any challenges I was experiencing. I was interested to learn about her plans for the staff and what strategies she would employ to improve the health of the residents in West and South Los Angeles. Dr. King was a dynamic supervisor who pushed me to think about public health in different ways. She stretched me above and beyond the role of health educator, gave me a lot of responsibility, and allowed me to find and develop my own strengths. One of the biggest responsibilities was creating a scope of work for West and South LA focused on health equity. No one in the department had ever attempted to take such an abstract concept like health equity and integrate it into the work of the staff in both service areas. Health equity looked so different in each of the service areas, which made the task quite challenging. South Central had so many needs that health equity was the most important issue to tackle, yet the most difficult to work on. In West Los Angeles, the need to address health equity was also there, but on a much smaller scale. The concerns were more localized to certain communities, such as Venice and Mar Vista. I was asked to put together a strategic plan for our community engagement work, assess the staff's readiness to provide culturally appropriate care to the LGBTQIA community, and design a training to better prepare them for the work. I participated in important initiatives such as the Health Committee of the Empowerment Congress, an organization created by a local legislator with the idea that government should be much more responsive to the needs of residents. The Empowerment Congress serves as a direct communication line from the community to the local legislator and is an opportunity to educate and inform the community about important public health topics. During my time there, we focused on issues such as trauma and violence prevention, health care access, HIV/AIDS, and the brand-new legal cannabis policies in the jurisdiction.

I also represented her at meetings with leadership and other high-level executives. It is quite a big deal to earn the trust and respect of a supervisor to the extent that they are comfortable sending you to speak on their behalf at high-profile meetings. I perceived her to be very forward thinking, something I admired and sought to emulate. She was the first person I ever heard mention the term "social determinants of health," and she tasked me with creating programs to help the staff and the community to understand this new, and quite abstract, concept that dealt with issues not health related at all—heavy-hitting issues such as poverty, educational attainment, housing, and employment. Incorporating attention to these issues into our work was quite difficult, as they are complex and time consuming to bring about change. Progress is often not seen for many years or even decades. This focus was different from the disease prevention and health education work we were all used to doing. These topics require sustained multi-sector collaboration to change policy and systems so that people have the chance to live healthy lives. If we can repair societal systems and get people out of poverty, into good schools, good housing, and good jobs, then we can guarantee that they will have a better standard of living, less disease, and longer life expectancy. Suddenly that queasy feeling I always got when driving through Malibu made perfect sense. It wasn't just about one community having more resources. Although that is a significant part of the problem, the magnitude of the problem was much bigger than that. The larger social structures that created and perpetuate poverty are the central issue at hand.

Dr. King was the first person in the entire department to push for more work on these issues as well as the impact of racism on population health. I learned so much from her leadership and guidance. She taught me that it's not enough to complain about a problem; it's important to have a solution-focused mindset as well. Dr. King went to bat for me many times while under her leadership and always supported my efforts to grow professionally. Her example has helped remind me to do the same for other women, especially women that look like me and come from communities like mine. On one occasion I was asked by a community partner to be present during a speech the mayor of Los Angeles was giving to highlight efforts the organization was making around cycling in South Central Los Angeles. I would not be speaking; I would just be present on the platform while the mayor spoke, and he would give comments about the work I had been doing to support the community bicycling program. I was so excited because I enjoyed the weekly bike rides the organization hosted that took us through the streets of South Central. I had made friends with the other cyclists and had started to bring my friends and even my dad along as well to join in on the fun.

My involvement in this effort was the catalyst to a 545-mile bike ride from San Francisco to LA that I did for AIDS LifeCycle in 2012. The ride is a fundraiser to provide treatment and other services for people with HIV and AIDS. The trip takes seven days and heads down the California coast. Over 2,000 cyclists make the trek each year, and that year I rode with a wonderful group of five women and had the privilege to see my home state in a different way. To go from weekly bike rides around the neighborhood to a 545-mile bike ride is a huge endeavor, and it was a very significant project that had a huge impact on my life. I was so excited, and per protocol, I told my boss, who then made the ask of the executive staff and our public affairs office. I was so excited about the possibility of participating.

A day or so later we found out that I wasn't allowed to attend the event. It was never really clear to me why the answer was no, it was just no and that was it. I could hear the resignation in her voice as she shared the details of the conversation and apologized to me. I hung up the phone, and for the first time since I began my County career, I cried softly at my desk, with my shawl on my face to hide the tears. I was so disappointed. All the hard work I was doing to be a public health ambassador was finally paying off, but then I was stopped from participating for seemingly no good reason. It didn't make sense. Dr. King realized how important this was and went back and advocated for me, and I was eventually given the okay to stand with the mayor during the press conference.

Dr. King was also a great example of leveraging potentially negative opportunities into positive ones. Since the beginning of my career in the West/South LA Regional Office, I was the only health educator for the entire region. Other offices had two health educators to share the work. I never understood why there was only one of me in a service area with some of the greatest need. South LA could have easily used two health educators alone! Why was I the only one trying to manage both offices? I was never given a clear answer, so I just continued to do my work as always. One day in 2012, I was told I would finally get a colleague to support the West LA service area. It turns out Dr. King had gotten into a bit of hot water for missing an important meeting due to other needs in the office. When asked to account for her absence, she was able to turn it into an opportunity to ask for more staff and they obliged. We had been asking for additional staff for many years, and she successfully took a situation that could have ended poorly and used it to her advantage.

When people you respect set high expectations for your life, you're compelled to meet them. All the women who shaped me professionally saw something in me and set out to nurture me, but the most important thing is that I had to believe I was capable of meeting and exceeding their vision for me.

Just as people have taught and mentored me, my public health career has allowed me to share my love of public health with others through teaching positions and mentoring opportunities for over a decade. In 2008, only a few years after I started my job as a health educator, I began teaching introductory health courses at Cal State University Los Angeles and the University of Phoenix. My teaching career was kicked off with the help of two colleagues, Jameelah my office mate who morphed into a family member, and Emma Fredua, a woman that I never worked with but met through our shared experience working in STD prevention at the department. Jameelah and I, both young mothers at the time, decided we needed to earn extra income. She brought up online teaching as an option. I was intrigued, so we both sent in applications to the University of Phoenix and landed teaching assignments right away. Emma was adjunct faculty at Cal State LA and reached out to me one day about teaching. There wasn't any specific opportunity that we were aware of at the time but we both devised a plan. She would email the faculty chair to introduce me. I would then respond with my interest in teaching and a brief review of my education and experience. Our plan worked and I was asked to submit my resume and apply for an adjunct faculty position. The support and encouragement of both women was valuable, but it's important to note that I had to do the work and prove myself credible, reliable, and knowledgeable. When you are ready, the opportunities almost always present themselves, but you have to do the work.

I taught at Cal State LA for four years and was asked to come back to teach in 2019. The classes I taught at Cal State LA and University of Phoenix were focused primarily on personal health topics, but I always sprinkled a little bit of public health into those classes. I wanted students to understand that taking care of their personal health is important, but that context is everything. One can only take care of their health to the extent that resources are available to do so. In class we talked a lot about communities without healthy food options and access to care. These same communities also happened to have lots of fast food options and liquor stores. How can someone eat better when there is literally no grocery store nearby to buy produce and several fast food restaurants within walking distance? Students have to understand the context by which they make health-promoting or health-damaging choices.

In 2014, I taught introductory public health courses at Occidental College and Ashford University. Again, the opportunity arose through a connection with a like-minded colleague I met while working in South LA. I have learned that when people bear witness to your work ethic, your commitment, and your passion, they will look out for you. Heng Lam Foong was a woman I worked with on a nutrition grant in the South Los Angeles office. She eventually left and went to work at Occidental College. When a need for an adjunct professor arose, she reached out and asked me to consider applying. She wanted to make sure that the perspective of women of color was present, especially in the field of public health. She felt strongly that the students would benefit from my perspective and experience. I would not have known such an opportunity was available if she hadn't shared it with me. I applied and was offered the position, which allows me the wonderful privilege of sharing public health from my unique corner of the universe with undergraduate students, some of whom have never had a black woman from South Los Angeles at the front of their classroom. They come from all over the US and the world with varying degrees of interest in public health, health administration, medicine, and public policy. I help the students understand how their lived experiences relate directly to their health outcomes and how those same concepts apply to their communities back home and at school. We don't get very far in class without explaining the prevention and community focus of the field as well as the impact that poverty and racism have on the health of entire communities. I also take the time to share my experiences as well, in school and as a teen mother. It's an important step in helping them to understand how public health works.

My hope is that they leave with a newfound love and respect for public health with a sprinkle of my very informed opinion of life as a black woman mixed in. As I learn new information about public health, I make sure to pass that information on to the students. I enjoy having the opportunity to share my unique blend of education and experience with students, many of whom have backgrounds and experiences very different from mine. Both online and in person, I have integrated teaching students about the very important foundation of public health into the fabric of my career.

I've helped students get jobs, fellowships, commission seats, and many other opportunities where they've expressed interest. One of the best stories ever is the time a graduate student from an online university met with me for an informational interview. She met me in my office, and we made small talk about the projects I was working on. I was heading to a community meeting that afternoon and, on a whim, asked her if she would like to go with me. She jumped at the chance and off we went to a meeting at the South Los Angeles Health Projects in Inglewood, California. We got to the meeting, I introduced her to everyone, and soon after the meeting began. As we made our way through the agenda, the facilitator expressed the need for a volunteer to assist with a project. The room grew quiet. No one likes to volunteer when there is so much other work that has to be done anyway. Everyone's face read "please don't make me do it" or "I hope she asks someone else." After a very lengthy pause, a response came.

"I'll do it," my guest said, raising her hand enthusiastically.

Not long after, she was hired full time by the agency and worked there for a few years before moving on to other opportunities.

Many other students have come to my office over the years, eager to learn about the work I do and how they can "get in" to begin their careers as well. I'm always happy to speak to them and share whatever information I have available. It's so important to share knowledge and experience with young people, especially when they are receptive and open to learning.

On another occasion I was invited to give a presentation to a student organization at USC. After the meeting, the president of the organization reached out and asked if there were any volunteer opportunities where could work with me. I didn't have anything available, and I was hesitant to take on a volunteer due to the time commitment, but in the end, I created an opportunity for the student and agreed to take him on. He was able to secure funding for his position and jumped right in, writing reports and taking care of a host of other responsibilities.

I started my public health career wanting to help people and ended up helping myself as well. Not only did I get a better understanding of the many issues impacting the communities I worked in and lived in, but I also gained colleagues and friends who have supported my professional career and pushed me further than I could have ever imagined. I can look at the bigger picture, both good and bad, in almost any situation, and think through strategies and solutions that can benefit all parties. I've learned important lessons like how to consider alternate points of view, how to be more compassionate, and ways to continuously work towards equity and eliminate injustice. Even though you may not be in the public health field like I am, there are always opportunities to get involved in your community to make it better for everyone. I encourage you to get connected with local causes that you believe in. You too can benefit from the very change you seek.

Chapter Eight

Loving Yourself First

As a successful, educated black woman surrounded by positive female role models, you would think I'd have high-caliber suitors knocking down my door, fighting for my attention. Unfortunately, that is not my testimony. I spent way too much time with unsuitable love interests before I finally woke up. I wish I had back some of that time wasted carrying on with men who were not ambitious, with no drive and no goals or aspirations. There was no mutual benefit to these interactions, only one-sided and selfish withdrawals from my emotional bank account. I share my truth so you can take a look at your own life and take stock. Sometimes the strongest and most independent women can have the hardest time picking the right partner because deep down they question their worthiness.

When we fail to look deeply at our own patterns of behavior, we will not create the vision of that which we want or need. We waste precious time that could be spent on our own self-development and growth when we pursue love interests who are not uplifting and encouraging and are instead disempowering and oppressive. If my words resonate with you, I challenge you to begin to analyze your thoughts and behaviors and make changes for the better. Settling for a man who is beneath you is relevant to every woman, but as a successful black woman, I see many of my friends settle for less in a man for a number of reasons: we believe the lie that there are not enough black men to go around, we buy into the notion that something is better than nothing, or we make a concerted effort not to discount black men because we understand and empathize with the many societal and economic pressures they face. These beliefs cause us to lose sight of our own needs in order to prove a point for the "greater good." Settling for less can be dangerous because it causes us harm in the end when the product of those bad decisions comes to light.

Part of my issue was my struggle with my plus size. I compensated for my "less than perfect figure" by being a people pleaser. I struggled with confidence in my own body and behaved in ways that I thought would make me likeable in the eyes of the men I was seeing. My battle with my weight hovered over me like a gray cloud for many years. During my last year in graduate school and before I started working in South LA, my mother pushed me to go to Lindora. I'd seen the Lindora commercials on television but didn't quite know what the program was all about. I called the number, spoke to a representative, and scheduled a consultation. On the day of the consultation, I drove to a generic office building in Culver City and spoke to a woman about the program. She shared her story of success and how she had lost a lot of weight and kept it off over the years. She was a very pretty, young black woman and I was very impressed with her and the benefits of the program. I signed up that day and eventually did two rounds of the program. I had to track all of my food and go in for daily weigh-ins and B12 injections. The diet was medically supervised, low carb/high protein, and designed to put the body into ketosis. It was pretty intense. The first few days of the program I could only eat foods high in protein. Every few hours I choked down special protein bars and other prepackaged foods, boiled eggs, chicken breasts, and anything low carb and high protein. After those first few days the meal plan provided a bit more balance, but it was hard not being able to eat bread or rice or other "normal" foods while everyone else was eating pizza and hamburgers. But I stuck it out, measuring portions and weighing my food. The program was very difficult, but it worked.

Over the course of several months I went from 212 pounds to 129 pounds. From a size 16 to a size 4. I was ecstatic and so proud of my accomplishment. I went shopping and bought an entirely new wardrobe. I got to shop in all the "normal" clothing stores and wear all the cute clothes. I was "normal"; I didn't take up too much space, and I was what society said I was supposed to be, a young and skinny girl.

I should've been happy with the weight loss, but I wasn't completely satisfied. I didn't like my shape, or myself, and so enter the unworthy guys who are mirrors of what I think of myself. This led to some pretty sketchy situations for me, like engaging in sexual relations before I was ready, or not asking important questions that would tease out important information such as their intentions for me or what type of person they really were. My sense of self-worth was often damaged by these negative interactions. My health was also impacted. After one brief encounter with a guy I met in my late twenties, I was told by my gynecologist that I had human papillomavirus, HPV, and would need surgery to remove lesions on my cervix. I was scared! I was familiar with the viral infection because in 2004, during a six-month stint at the STD Program as a health education assistant, I worked on an HPV research study at one of the public health centers. I had to enroll women in the study and ask them questions about risk factors such as number of sex partners they had before they went in to get tested for HPV. From my work on the study I knew that HPV was the most common sexually transmitted infection and that there was a strong link between HPV infection and cervical cancer. It was scary to think that something I had could give me cancer. I was so nervous on the day of the surgery. I had to wait several hours in the hospital waiting room before being wheeled in for the procedure. I was anxious and afraid. I cried and paced and worried. I wanted out of there, but I had to have the procedure to prevent any future risk of cancer.

For years after the surgery I went through a repeating cycle of Pap test, abnormal result, colposcopy. The Pap tests were painful and colposcopy exams were equally traumatizing. The colposcopy starts like a regular Pap test with a speculum, and then a vinegar solution is swabbed on the vaginal area, which burns. Then a biopsy is done, where the doctor literally takes a tiny piece of cervical tissue to send to a lab. It felt terrible. This happened every three to six months for many years. I waited and hoped for the virus to go away on its own so that I wouldn't have to go through the procedures anymore. I even asked my doctor if I could have a hysterectomy. In my mind, if I didn't have a cervix, I couldn't get cervical cancer. The doctor refused, saying I was too young. I was finally given a clean bill of health in my late thirties. Not taking the time to properly vet potential suitors can have devastating consequences. The amount of time and energy I spent to make sure I didn't get cervical cancer and the amount of pain, stress, and worry could have easily been avoided.

And even then, going through this agonizing pain of an unwanted STD that could have caused cancer, I still didn't align my mind, body, and spirit. I decided that liposuction was the new answer to my problem. I was excited because this was my chance, after all these years, to have the body I wanted. I thought it would make me feel better and place me closer to what I thought I was supposed to look like based on the many unrealistic messages women receive regularly about their bodies. I wanted an hourglass figure with no stomach and slender thighs, and liposuction was the way to make it happen. I decided to move forward with the procedure. I decided not to tell my parents what I was doing because I knew if I did, I would be met with resistance and judgment. I did not want to be talked out of my decision, so I simply kept it to myself. The surgery had a hefty price tag. Ten thousand dollars is a lot of money to spend on anything, much less plastic surgery. Without any hesitation I opened a credit account to cover the cost. The day of the procedure, my brother drove me to the office, and he picked me up afterwards. I expected him to give me a hard time about my choice, but he didn't; he just did what I asked. I suppose he thought that I knew what was best and understood that the choice was mine to make. He was the only person who knew what I was doing. That didn't last very long though. Once I got home and began my recovery it was impossible to keep the secret. Once my mom found out, she was livid. She didn't understand why I did it, which is why I didn't tell her in the first place. During my recovery I received a card in the mail from my aunt on my dad's side saying that I was perfect already and didn't need surgery. She had heard the news and the card was her way of letting me know she cared.

Although the liposuction provided some results, I had an unrealistic expectation of what the procedure could do for me. I thought once the surgery was done, life would be great, but it didn't quite turn out that way. One thing I looked forward to after surgery was getting into a favorite pair of jeans. I knew my body needed time to heal, so I didn't try them on right away, but after some time had passed, I thought I was ready. I pulled the jeans from my closet, stepped into them and began pulling them up. They were too small. I didn't understand why they didn't fit. I had just gotten liposuction; my body should be perfect. I pulled and tugged, trying to get them on, to no avail. I was so disappointed I started to cry. I hated that my body wasn't doing what I wanted it to do. Over time I calmed down and began to focus on other things, but that moment was yet another indication of how hard the fight was to achieve this idealized version of myself. Looking back, I don't regret having liposuction, but there were certainly a million other things I could have done with ten thousand dollars, like purchase property, open a business, or pay down my student loan debt. My mind was focused on issues that weren't important at all.

For many years after the surgery I struggled to keep my weight down. I would do my own bootleg Lindora program. I would eat lots of boiled eggs, veggie burger patties topped with vegetarian cheese, and other high-protein snacks to try to keep the pounds from coming back. I spent so much time trying to stay a certain weight that it became overwhelming. My coworkers thought I was crazy with all my strange food combinations. I still catch a lot of flak from Jameelah about my horrible-smelling vegetarian "burger" patty and vegan cheese combination that she was subjected to in that tiny office we shared. When my bootleg Lindora plan stopped working, I switched to Weight Watchers. That worked for a while, but after some time, even that stopped working. I got to a point where I was dieting so much that my body stopped responding. The scale just simply stopped moving. My metabolism was ruined. I was frustrated and certain that no one understood what I was going through. Most of my friends at the time were smaller than I was. They didn't have to eat weird combinations of food and step on the scale every day. It seemed so unfair.

The irony is not lost on me that I worked in public health while I was struggling with my weight, body image, and self-esteem. My coworkers probably knew more about what was happening with me than they ever cared to know, but to me this was an opportunity to garner support and encouragement through a particularly difficult season. At the time, much of the public health rhetoric regarding physical activity and nutrition focused on individual behavior change instead of broader change of the physical and social environment. Although individual behavior change can be very important for better health, it doesn't do much to shift the health of the community. In other words, a person may want to eat healthier and exercise more often, but if there are no grocery stores or safe parks to walk or play tennis, it makes it harder to adopt those new habits both individually and collectively. If a person must choose between taking two or three buses to get to the grocery store or walking down the block to get a burger and fries, the person is likely to make the choice that is most convenient for them. That doesn't mean that person is bad or that the choice is bad; it just means that public health and other organizations need to work to make the healthier option the easiest one so that more people choose it first and choose it often. I saw this very scenario play out in many different iterations in my neighborhood and the larger South LA community. On any major intersection in the community there are plenty of fast food restaurants and liquor stores, but not many grocery stores. We are just now at a place where we are starting to see cafes and sandwich shops and other businesses selling healthier food options. Corner stores in the neighborhood sell soda, alcohol, cigarettes, and maybe some canned food, but not much else. There were only one or two farmer's markets in the entire area.

Things got so bad that in 2008 the City Council placed a moratorium on fast food restaurants in South Central to try to balance the food options in the neighborhood and reduce obesity. Unfortunately, the plan did not work. If there are already a million fast food restaurants in the area, prohibiting one more from opening doesn't really change the food landscape very much. The moratorium was a day late and a dollar short, as the old folks say. The topic of overweight and obesity is a very tricky one. Much of the focus is usually on individual food choices, but there are so many factors that play a role in whether or not someone is overweight or obese. In my case, I believe that my weight is primarily determined by my genes along with my social environment and the food access in my community, which shaped my food preferences. Stress and trauma also play a significant role as well. Fast food isn't necessarily an enemy in low-income communities. It is a necessary food source for those that don't have access to a kitchen and can be a quick source of calories for busy families. The problem is the lack of balance in the types of food establishments prevalent in my community and others like mine.

Once again, my support system of black women colleagues set the tone for me. When I started my career in South Central, Martina and Dee not only nurtured me professionally, they served as examples in other areas of my life. I witnessed them lead very active and full lives while embracing vegetarianism. They talked a lot about their morning jogs around the park and their vegetarian lifestyle. They didn't tell me to take up running or to stop eating meat, but their lives were the perfect embodiment of leading by example. I wanted to try what they were doing because they were excellent representations of the outcome: a healthy life in older adulthood. I adopted a vegetarian and ultimately vegan diet and even tried my hand at running many years later because of the example they set forth.

This was the next level of change for me in my relationship with food. It was refreshing to see healthy, socially conscious older black women as role models who looked at food as integral to their lives but were not obsessed with numbers on a scale. Thinking needs to shift on a much broader scale if we want to see lasting changes in the health of communities. Because of their example, I tried vegetarianism and found that the world didn't fall apart after I gave up my last animal protein of choice which was chicken. I would later come to embrace a plant-based lifestyle, forgoing all meat, dairy, and cheese.

I got tired of fighting my body. I was at war with myself instead of learning to love myself. Besides, every time I gained weight, my body went right back to a size 14/16, as if it were trying to tell me where it wanted to be. I was finally starting to listen to my body and pay attention to what it needed. For many people wearing a size 16 after being as small as a size 4 would be devastating and disappointing, but in many ways, it was validating for me. I had come full circle, and that was okay.

I felt comfortable in my own skin, and I was no longer fighting myself tirelessly. I could take all that time spent obsessing about my body and apply it to my career, romance, friends, and learning more about myself. I finally reached a tipping point in my late thirties when I realized the question with men wasn't "Why don't they didn't value me?" The real question was "Why don't I value myself enough to want more?" I no longer wanted the interactions with men of my early twenties, which ran the spectrum from fly by night to "situationships" that lasted many months or even years that weren't heading anywhere. I wasted a lot of valuable time in my twenties wondering what was wrong with me, and why men didn't see enough value in me to want to commit. I would ask them why we weren't in a "real" relationship, and each and every time, the answer was a variation on a theme that ultimately meant "you're not worthy."

Without knowing the term, I was finally embarking on my own personal journey to body positivity. I was born to be this shape and size just like millions of other people are born to be their shape and size. I stopped assigning value and worth to weighing less. If you are eating well, getting fresh air and moving your body, doing a job you enjoy, and have good friends, then you can love yourself as you are regardless of size. Even if you are doing none of these things, you can still love yourself as you are. Moving into that frame of mind is not as easy as flipping a switch, but no one is judging you as much as you and if they are, they are likely fighting their own battle of poor self-image. Dieting causes us to eat in a way that is truly dysfunctional. The unnatural focus on eliminating carbs, sugar, or fat, or eating weird combinations of food, or elimination of entire types of food is so limiting. We convince ourselves that the restrictions are temporary and that we can "go back to normal" after the weight is off, but all that does is create a harmful relationship with food and our bodies. Not to mention it can cause a lot of damage to your mental health and sense of self.

I tell on myself to help you, so you don't feel alone in the same thought patterns. For example, during work meetings, if there are snacks, my attention constantly shifts to the food while everyone else is focused on the work. During family-style dining with friends or family, I will make note of how many pieces of food we each got so that no one gets more than the other, and I get a bit anxious about making sure I get what I perceive to be my fair share, as though there won't be enough to go around. I don't often notice other people around me doing this, but perhaps you experience this kind of food anxiety. If so, or you experience a different kind of stress about the foods you eat, sharing in a community and speaking out helps. We don't talk much as a culture about food in this way, and the dialogue needs to be more open.

The root of my low self-worth began when my relationship with Andréa's father failed. I was so sure that we would be together and raise our daughter. When that did not happen, it was a serious blow to my self-worth and put me in a very bad place. As time passed and I eventually moved on, dating as a single mother became quite an interesting endeavor. When Andréa was born my self-esteem was already low due to long-standing body image issues. The drama of co-parenting most certainly had an impact on my stress levels and undoubtedly impacted my weight. Although teen pregnancy was far from an anomaly in the late '90s, I approached dating with the assumption that no man would want to marry me, much less date me, and have to raise someone else's kid. While in college I hoped to find a suitable mate to marry, as I assumed every college age woman hoped for, but there was no time to attend parties or date. Besides, at the time, the black male population was so small at USC, the pickings were slim. Add in that I didn't live on campus and therefore didn't have the benefit of time and proximity to get to know many of my classmates. This had a profound impact on the quality of men that I chose and even how I selected the men that I dated through my late thirties. Although my ability to pick men wasn't very good, the custody arrangements that my daughter's father and I agreed on did allow me the opportunity to date and to have a personal life. I just didn't know who I was quite yet, which meant my choice of men reflected that uncertainty.

It might not feel like it at the time, but it's a tremendous blessing when that one relationship comes along that pushes you over the edge, that provides the loudest wakeup call ever and forces you to reevaluate your life and your values. I was thirty-eight, and finally in a very good place with my body. I had surrendered trying to be someone else, and so I thought I was really in sync with what I wanted. I was dating a man who was a friend of a friend, so right off the bat there was some unearned trust on my part just from association. He was about ten years older than I was, easy to talk to, very charismatic, and a great dresser with a sexy salt-and-pepper goatee. Does this type of man sound familiar to you? His children were grown, as was my daughter, so there were no childcare concerns, and he also had a lot of free time, which meant that I got the attention that I craved. The downside was that he had so much free time because he didn't have a real job. My 9-to-5 working woman self with two college degrees spent all my free time with a man with a high school diploma and no job. I don't know how I convinced myself that he was a suitable companion; when I think about it, I just shake my head in disbelief.

And here is what is so crazy about all this. He was very critical of my body, to the point that plastic surgery was brought up frequently. I was finally at the point where I was accepting of who I was and the body I lived in, so to have this issue come up again made me radically uncomfortable in my skin, and I look back now and see that this was the final test of my will to truly love myself and say "no more" to bad men. The final frontier before my forties. He kept me ironically "small" and hidden away because he was a very skillful liar and a cheater. He was seeing another woman when he met me, and he conveniently forgot to stop seeing her once we got involved. I didn't know any of this until the very end of the relationship when the evidence became insurmountable. Although I didn't know he was cheating on me until the end of our relationship, I had many clues that he was not good for me that I consciously ignored so I wouldn't lose my crutch. The first clue that he wasn't the right man for me occurred on our very first date. We went to a new vegan Ethiopian restaurant for lunch in a food court just east of USC. The food is prepared cafeteria style, so you walk up, point to what you want, they place it on a platter, and you pay for it and get your food. When it was time to pay, I did the dance that all women do in our minds: I gracefully stepped back to allow him to pay, but I was also ready to pay for my own meal if necessary. I noticed that he also was hesitating. I was confused. I quickly realized that he was not planning to pay for our meal. I am far from a gold digger or opportunist, but I was taught that a man pays for the date, especially the first one. That first date should have been our last. It's not fair to try to pursue someone when your finances are not in order. It was very rude and inconsiderate for him to assume that I would pay for both of us. Unfortunately, I went right along with it, paying for all our dates and activities over the years.

As our time together continued, I often complained to him that I felt "hidden." We would go out quite often, but I was not introduced to family, and I was not mentioned on his social media channels. In fact, in some instances, I was intentionally omitted from his postings of events and outings that he and I attended together, most of which I financed. It made sense during the first year of dating when we were still "new" and trying to determine if we were a good fit for each other, but going into the second year, it didn't make sense anymore and became very frustrating and outright insulting. I am a beautiful woman who deserves to be shown off and adored by a fully engaged and interested partner. I wrestled with the disconnect but continued to see him. How many of us get very clear signs that we are not being valued and yet continue to entertain an unhealthy relationship?

One of the final straws was Valentine's Day 2017. He was mysteriously silent for most of the day. There was no "Happy Valentine's Day" text or phone call, no surprise delivery of flowers at work. Nothing. I simmered in anger for the entire morning. By one p.m., I was at my wits' end and fired off a series of angry texts. He apologized and came by later, but after the breakup I found out where he was that day. The other woman had taken him out and spent a large amount of money the night before on a romantic getaway.

My instincts told me all of this was wrong, that I deserved more than what I was getting, and that something was up, but I put up with it anyway. When it all came to light, feeling hidden made perfect sense. I was being shielded from the other woman and kept away from people who would likely warn me about what was going on.

I found out about the indiscretion in the craziest way. Someone made the effort to type and mail five anonymous letters to my home over the course of several months. The letters contained very specific, detailed information about the person I was seeing and the double life he was leading. Someone was looking out for me, trying to save me from this horrible situation. Although the contents of the letters were very informative, the experience was extremely traumatizing. For quite a while I'd arrive home and be seized with fear as I approached my mailbox, wondering if another letter with no return address would be there. Here I was, smart, successful, a board member, an adjunct professor, a property owner with lots of friends, and scared to look in my own mailbox. Those letters prompted me to do my own research into the relationship. I uncovered all the lies and ultimately confronted him. It was amazing to hear him "confess" to specific incidents and situations, only to find out later that the confessions were more lies and half-truths. You would think that would have been the end of it, but I continued to see him for several more months before finally breaking it off. I spoke to the other young lady directly before I acted.

How many of us get the hypothetical "letter" in the mail? The call to action that warns us that a relationship is detrimental to our mental and physical health? It may not be an actual letter like the ones I received, but we are often given many clues that the person we are seeing is not the best for us, and we ignore them. I hung on to a harmful relationship for much longer than I should have and kept going when the evidence was clear that I should leave. I could say that I'm not sure why I did it, but the reality is that my sense of self was gone. I didn't trust my instincts and I thought that having a smidgen of something, even if it was bad, was better than having nothing at all. My rational mind knows better than to think that way, but having the attention of a man who found me desirable caused me to waver in ways that I know weren't good for me.

Picking the right life partner is so important for several reasons. We thrive when we have strong social networks and support systems. We are often healthier and have a better quality of life when we have a compatible partner that provides strong social and emotional support. Then there are the economic benefits to partnering up, such as pooled resources, higher income, access to health care, and the ability to build generational wealth that can be unattainable for many people without a partner.

When we pick the wrong partner, as I had done for so many years, unnecessary pain can have very real health consequences such as sexually transmitted disease, poor mental health, and depression. I am very lucky to currently have a strong social support system that I wish I'd had in my twenties. My current group of friends rallied around me and offered me support and encouragement during the end of the horrible relationship. They didn't judge me but listened to my story and were there when I needed them the most.

The inner work on myself at a deeper level drove the decision to no longer be a victim. I was guilty of believing I wasn't worthy of love and respect. Guilty of thinking that my weight meant that I had to settle for whoever came my way. Guilty of not being brave enough to verbalize what I wanted and expected from a relationship, and thinking if I just act the way I think they want me to act, and behave the way they want me to, everything will work out.

As a result of this very important time of reflection, I took some important steps. I wrote a letter thanking him for all that he had done, from cutting down the overgrown trees in the front yard, to teaching me that I am worth more and deserve more. After the letter was complete, I burned it in the presence of my daughter, allowing those words to disappear into the universe never to be seen again. This was a nod to my love of ceremony and pomp and circumstance, and an acknowledgment of this transition. We laughed and shrieked as the letter flew out of my daughter's hands, caught by a gust of wind. It was a fitting moment of closure to a terrible ordeal. I loved the opportunity to share with my daughter how to hold yourself in higher value when picking your romantic partners. That it is okay to make mistakes, in fact, it's essential in order to gain self-trust.

I also took the opportunity to learn. I took a dating class with other Type A black women and signed up for a professional matchmaking service. If I was going to break the cycle, I had to learn what I wanted in a partner, what I did not want, and how to date for marriage. The matchmaker only provided me with one halfway decent guy out of the three dates, but it was still fun and enlightening to go on dates and be shown a good time. I had missed so much for so many years by accepting less than I deserved that it felt weird to go on a proper date and have my meal and drinks paid for.

Self-reflection coupled with the classes and the matchmaker changed my reality. I was open and ready to see what life had to offer on the dating scene. I told everyone who mattered that I was single and ready to date. I was putting my intentions into the universe and projecting an attitude of contentment and confidence, and it paid off. I met an amazing man who compliments me. We share a love for social justice, community, and culture and truly enjoy each other's company. We even have the same diet; both of us are vegans and have been for many years now. There was mutual respect and a desire to get to know each other deeply, beyond any physical attraction, which was very important to me.

As women, we are much more than the sum of our parts. We are inherently flawed, but in that imperfection is the essence of who we are. We need to be patient and forgiving with ourselves and let go of the unrealistic expectations that society places on us and the ones that we place on ourselves. We can do everything right: graduate from college, get a good job, date all the right men, and still not be happy and content with ourselves. It's important for women to get together and be open and transparent about our experiences so that we no longer have to carry any burden by ourselves. We can offer a hand up to other women so that they can avoid the traps we've fallen in and elevate themselves. Most importantly, we must pass this knowledge on to our daughters, sisters, and other young women we come across. We must work to create a new culture of connectedness, a new way of thinking that embraces collective care and concern in this current age of increased isolation and independence. This new way of engagement not only benefits and lifts up women, it also creates healthier families and communities for everyone.

Chapter Nine

When It All Starts to Connect

From the time my daughter was born, I've marveled at this funny bit of mathematics: when my daughter reached twenty-one years old, I wouldn't even be forty yet! I'd be the parent of an adult child and still be young enough to get out there and do what I wanted to do with my life. No more custody and visitation issues, no more shuffling her back and forth between two homes, and no more arguments with her dad. The thought of all the stress going away made me happy and kept me going when things would inevitably get rough during those years co-parenting. I'm certain my stress levels have dropped exponentially now that the extraordinary, seemingly impossible coordination needed during those days are over. I'm happier, more self-assured, and maintain a very strong relationship with my daughter. As I approached forty, I began to reflect on my life. Forty is a good stopping place for all of us women to look back at the various versions of ourselves. I've gone through so many iterations—the chubby kid who was smart but had low self-esteem; the teen mom who pushed through despite the challenges with school and family; the young woman who looked for validation and love externally, only to be met with disappointment; and the woman who raised her child. I was entering a new phase in life where the focus was finally on self. The benefit of looking back is that I can shed light on the issues that women of all ages in their various stages of life encounter. My hope is that there is some benefit from the many lessons I've learned, and inspiration to act.

Society talks a lot about the negative aspects of pregnant and parenting teens, such as decreased educational and economic opportunities, and they are very important issues for sure, but they don't talk about the positives. Being "done" with raising my child while everyone else is just starting out is certainly one of them. I might have missed out on the partying and traveling as a teen mom, but I can do all that now, and I can actually afford and appreciate it! Also, because of the support of my family all those years ago, I was able to avoid some of the major pitfalls that often hurt teen parents, such as having to drop out of school while raising my daughter. I was able to secure economic stability for us, which allowed me to buy my first home as a single mother with one income, attend graduate school, and buy income property. I'm not trivializing the many issues that impact pregnant and parenting teens as they try to navigate through society while raising their children, but with the proper support from family and community, along with resources such as childcare assistance, housing assistance, and educational and career counseling, pregnant and parenting teens can succeed.

The most valuable lesson I learned in raising my daughter young was patience, with my daughter, with others, and with myself. When I was younger, I wanted life to hurry up so bad. I wanted to be an adult and be on my own. I doubt that I am the only one who felt this way growing up, but having a child early certainly sped up a lot of life's lessons. I had to grow up quickly and take on more responsibility that I know I wasn't ready for, but over the years, I learned to slow down, to be patient, to wait and see and not worry so much about what's next. Other lessons that I had no choice but to learn were persistence, to keep learning, and to work around people when they refuse to work with you. That last one was so important. Trying to co-parent taught me very quickly that people will place roadblocks in your life, intentionally or not, and those roadblocks often have nothing to do with me and everything to do with their own issues and insecurity. The skill is to find the work-around, the strategy or method to make things happen while avoiding that person and their issues completely. I've used the work-around many times in my life, from trying to figure out how to get my child to school when her father was unwilling or unable to do so to successfully navigating supervision challenges at work. The work-around saves a lot of time and energy. Instead of arguing with someone and trying to convince them to act in the way you want them to, you pivot and work around them. They are free to continue to think and feel the way they wish, and you are free to get what you want accomplished. These skills have been so helpful from the time I gained my independence from my parents to the day my daughter left home in her late teens.

Andréa moved away at age eighteen and did a pretty good job of forging her own path. She made some mistakes, as young adults often do; the pit bull that she decided to get while living in a cramped apartment with two roommates (one owned a cat) was a huge one. But the best thing about it all is that we talk it through, and she ultimately arrives at a solution that works for her. Of course, a mother's work is never really done, but it did change quite a bit as she got older. The dynamic between us shifted. I will always be her mother, guiding her through life and offering insight and direction when needed, but now I'm also her friend. We go shopping together (I still pay for almost everything though), we talk about the latest makeup trends and what products I should try, and trade tips on hair care. We talk about grown-up stuff like how to nail a job interview, how she should handle co-worker drama at work, or how to talk to her friends when there are disagreements.

I often see many moms lament the fact that their children have flown the coop. I don't doubt that empty nest syndrome is a real thing;

I just never experienced it. I wasn't sad that Andréa left. She's supposed to grow up and leave, and if I'm lucky, she won't come back. She's supposed to figure out how to wash her own clothes and pay her own bills and find a job and all the other things that grown-ups do. She doesn't belong to me. She belongs to herself and has to learn to listen to herself and do what's best for her. Part of my job now as the parent of an adult child is to help her learn to trust her own instincts, to act with integrity, and find her voice. The best way that any parent can do these things is to lead by example as well as offer insight and perspective to help their children navigate their newfound independence. I challenge all mothers, especially those who are finding it difficult to adjust to their new role as mothers of adult children, to find ways to re-focus on the things that brought happiness and satisfaction before. As mothers it's very easy to lose ourselves in our children. Once they grow up and leave, we're sometimes left to wonder "what's next?" As women, it's important to carve out time for ourselves for self-care and personal development so that boredom and depression don't kick in when our children leave.

When she left home, I didn't leave her room untouched as some shrine to a child that's grown up and moved on. I pulled the carpet up, laid down a nice hardwood floor, bought some lighting, a backdrop, and a camera, and officially upgraded a lifelong fashion hobby into a business.

As a plus-size woman, I make it my responsibility to show other plus-size women in my age range that they can dress well without breaking the bank. I'm also an advocate of breaking the fashion rules that are placed on larger women. We're often told to stay away from bright colors, stripes, and loud patterns. I almost always wear bright colors, love stripes, and loud patterns are my best friend, especially animal print. My blog, Style Vicksen, includes posts on Instagram and YouTube videos of my outfits and nail looks. I learned how to record and edit my own videos and take my own fashion and nail photos. Those early blog posts, photos, and videos weren't very good at all, but as time passed my content got better and I began to create partnerships with plus-size brands and other plus-size bloggers. I also began to realize the importance of shopping local and developed relationships with local businesses owned by black women. I hosted pop-up shops and clothes swaps in my backyard to build a sense of community and to inspire people to support the local economy and reduce the amount of clothes in landfills. It's amazing to be able to build a small community of like-minded people and watch it grow.

I also was able to participate in the Women's Policy Institute, a program aimed at developing leaders in public policy. I was pushed to apply by one of my good friends, who participated the year before. My application was initially denied, but funding was made available to the organization and I was asked to participate. I was grateful for the opportunity to attend trainings and workshops in Sacramento with a cohort of twenty women from all over the state. In a year's time, I drafted health care policy with five of these women and worked to push the policy through the legislative process. It was a lot of hard work, but it was very exciting to see the legislative process at work. Our bill was signed into state law by Governor Brown in 2014.

I also played a small part in helping a first-time candidate win a seat for the council district I live in. It felt good to help raise money and support the campaign headquarters in order to get the councilmember elected. I was so inspired by his win that I emailed him soon afterwards to congratulate him and ask how I could assist in continuing the work he envisioned for the community. I wasn't sure where that email would land me, but I knew that it was important to take a chance and ask for what I wanted, even if I wasn't exactly sure what the results would be. I ran into him at a community event soon after where we were both speaking. After he spoke, I stopped to say hello and make small talk. His first words to me were, "I'm appointing you to the City Health

Commission." I was ecstatic! I thanked him for the opportunity and tried my hardest not to smile like a big cheeseball. Hard to believe this teen mom twenty years later was looking at such an accomplishment!

At our first commission meeting, I met the fourteen other commissioners who represented the other council districts across the city. The first order of business was to determine our governing structure. We decided on a president and two vice presidents. I was itching to serve as one of the two vice presidents and nominated myself immediately. I was very surprised when no one seconded my nomination, effectively ending my short bid to hold a leadership position on the commission. My ego was a bit bruised, but I learned an important lesson that day about relationships and connections. I went into the meeting knowing who I was and what I was capable of, but no one else knew. I needed to spend time developing relationships with the commissioners and earn their trust and respect. I was patient and continued to serve, and my efforts paid off. Some months later, the president of the commission, a former council member from West LA, passed away. This caused a vacancy for second vice president. I put my hat in the ring once again and was voted into the role of second vice president. The following year, I was elected chair and served in this capacity for two terms. I had never been part of a commission, much less a brand-new one. Public service is something that I feel is an important responsibility. I am grateful for the opportunity to help my community and am very glad that I had the wherewithal to reach out and ask the councilmember how I could lend my support. He provided me an opportunity that I was able to take full advantage of.

Being a commissioner is a different type of public service. As chair I was often yelled at during public comment or called out of my name. Those moments can be difficult because it feels like a personal attack. I've learned that public service can be quite challenging, but the goal is always the same: to work on behalf of residents to make things better.

Besides, I have been through a lot of personal conflict in my life. I have learned I have a tough skin, and now I can apply that backbone to make change.

A few years later, another opportunity to connect with like-minded black women fell right into my lap. One evening in 2017 I arrived very early to a volunteer recognition event being hosted by the mayor of Los Angeles. I was so early that there was only one other person in the room. I immediately went over to greet her. She introduced herself as Celestine Palmer and handed me a card that read "LAAWPAC." The name looked very familiar. "Is LAAWPAC related to LAAWPPI in some way?" I asked her. It turns out I was speaking to the creator of the Los Angeles African American Women's Public Policy Institute! I was thrilled and realized very quickly that this was my opportunity to "apply" to the program in person. I spent the entire evening with Ms. Palmer, sharing my work experience, my community work, and my goals and aspirations. Ms. Palmer introduced me to her friends and colleagues and shared her knowledge and experience with me. It was an amazing evening. I made sure to apply to the program, went in for an interview, and was subsequently admitted into the program. The connections I made with the twenty-plus women in my cohort have been amazing and life changing. Proving, once again, that black women not only get along, we can connect and make magic happen whenever our paths cross.

I was so busy and had so many exciting ideas about my life. My plate was full, and I was completely preoccupied with these new avenues in my life, but in the back of my mind I worried about what my daughter planned to do with her life. Still maintaining the boundary of her making her own self-affirming decisions, I did step in to talk to her about leaving college after one semester. I didn't give her a hard time about it, but I did check in often, asking, "You going to summer school?" The answer was always "yes," but the action didn't follow. I trusted that she would figure it out eventually. I got some pushback from a few colleagues and friends who meant well. Many of them wanted me to force her to finish school. They told me I should "put my foot down" and "let her know who's boss." I didn't feel the need to do so. For one, I was sure that my daughter already felt bad enough about what had happened. After all, I had financed her entire education, taking out a loan to pay tuition and fees. It was my pocketbook on the line, not hers, so I'm sure she felt terrible about not following through. Being hard on her would not change that. Secondly, she was already an adult and was free to decide for herself when and how she would like to proceed with schooling and any other aspect of her life. My job was to offer support, encouragement, and advice when asked. She ultimately decided to work for some time before trying to go back to school. She expressed an interest in studying for a career as an esthetician, but in the meantime, she'd enter the workforce. She is skilled at getting jobs but learned very quickly that jobs in retail are grossly underpaid and cannot sustain life in expensive Los Angeles. It was an important lesson for her and an opportunity for me to continue preaching my "finish school" sermon whenever she'd whine about low pay and hard work. I could only step back so much.

There are realities to face in today's economy. Times are much harsher now than when I was younger or when my parents were coming of age. Everything is expensive; jobs don't offer the same type of financial stability and sense of security as they did before. She was going to have to figure out how to earn a decent living in an economy that does not pay people without advanced degrees very well. Her challenge is going to be how to thrive in a society that is harsh and unforgiving.

Without a shadow of a doubt, I did the absolute best I could raising Andréa. I think most parents do the best they can. Many parents are saddled with the dysfunction and trauma of their own childhoods and often don't have the time or resources to reflect on the impact those experiences have on them as parents. I was acutely aware of the many issues that impacted me growing up such as body image and poor self-esteem, and I made sure not to project them on Andréa. I believe this is why we are so close and communicate so well. I never wanted Andréa to feel bad about herself and her body. I recognized early on that society would show and tell her in many ways that she was "less than" as a plus-size black girl. It was my job to build her up and speak life into her, especially because of my own experiences as an overweight child. I owed that to her.

I often encounter young mothers raising young children. I see myself in them and always try to provide support and encouragement. There are three things that I always tell them:

1. It gets better with time.

The frustration, the arguments and the emotion involved with co-parenting are very real, but with time, growth, and maturity, those issues that seemed so big suddenly don't matter anymore. What matters most is that the child you share is loved and cared for and has everything they need to thrive. Everything else is secondary.

2. The more love and support the child has, the better.

Often parents get upset when the other parent moves on and starts a new relationship. Or perhaps the mother is concerned about the amount of time the father's parents or other relatives are spending with the child. it's very important for the child to be loved on and supported by as many people as possible. The child will benefit greatly and flourish from the love and support of everyone in the family. Trying to control or hinder positive relationships can be very harmful to the child emotionally as well as economically. Raising children can be very costly, and removing or limiting their time with family members can keep them from much-needed funds from extended family for childcare, after-school programs, school supplies, and other things. My family benefitted greatly from the large circle of love around me and my younger brother. Our schooling was fully financed by my great-grandparents. So on top of the love we received, we were also able to attend great schools and have many of our needs met through our extended family.

3. Self-care is very important.

A lot of young mothers put their entire focus on their children and don't allow themselves time to relax or focus on their own personal growth or what makes them happy. I've seen moms neglect themselves in ways that rob them of working on their physical health, self-care, and intimate relationships. It's impossible to be a good mom if you're not taking care of yourself. Also, children learn self-awareness and self-care by watching their parents.

In my work, I often advise women to exercise, eat healthy, get regular Pap tests, not smoke, and drink water instead of soda. As I've gained more knowledge and experience in public health, I recognize how patronizing these messages can be because they often don't address people's very complicated lives. What often doesn't get discussed is what I've heard referred to as the "urgency of now," the idea that people are too busy dealing with their immediate needs to focus on adopting new ideas and concepts, even if those ideas and concepts would be helpful to them in some way. When I was young, I felt like there was plenty of time to get my life together or do the things I wanted to do. Now, at age forty, there just isn't enough time in the day. It's not just a poor ability to manage time that's the problem. Our entire society is running too fast. In other words, what is happening right now is more important than working to prevent something that may or may not happen later. It's an important survival mechanism for many, especially women who may be just trying to make it through the day. What would be more helpful to women is stronger support networks, more resources to care for children or adult parents so that they are freed to pursue work or other economic and social interests. These resources can be life changing for women and help them move beyond the urgency of now, focus on realizing their dreams, and achieve them. In turn, they can help the next generation of women seek and maintain healthier relationships with their partners and their children. My suggestion for women is to work to create those support networks I mentioned previously. They are an important aspect of self-care and provide a strong safety net amidst all the daily stressors. If you're not sure about how to create a support network, please look for community organizations and social organizations that are in line with your current interests. There are likely to be women there who are open to providing support and encouragement.

Another strategy to integrating self-care into your life is scheduling it in just like any other appointment. For me, nail polish and nail art are an important part of my self-care. It's an opportunity to be creative and to be still (so I don't mess up my manicure). No matter how busy I get, I take the time every weekend to settle down and paint my nails. Find a hobby that makes you happy, and schedule the time to do it. It can be something very small such as keeping a journal or writing a letter to a friend, or something active, like taking a walk or riding a bicycle. Whatever it is, integrate it into your weekly routine as if your life depended on it.

Women have a unique perspective and a unique voice that can provide much-needed perspective and nuance on community solutions that can change lives for the better. It has taken some time for me, but I finally came to terms with my role as a leader and the importance of being a connector, someone who brings people and resources together. I also found value in my voice as a black woman, public health advocate, educator, and former teen mother.

This phase of my life has been so rewarding. I've learned so much about myself and have had the opportunity to focus on things that I love doing, develop new relationships, and work to improve my community. Being a mother has been a wonderful experience unlike any other I've had, and having the chance to develop a deeper relationship with my adult daughter has been so meaningful. This new chapter of my life, where I focus on who I am and what I want to do, is equally rewarding.

Chapter Ten

How Healthy Are Our Opinions?

A phenomenon I see quite often in many communities is the inability to consider differing opinions or alternate points of view. When different opinions are expressed, the immediate response is that the person is hateful or combative. This is troubling because many of the problems in our community today, from our relationships with others to much larger community-level issues such as poverty and violence, stem from making snap judgments, relying on surface level information, or simply refusing to consider that there is another way to think of an issue.

Take religion.

Despite my decision to live a secular life, I credit my Christian upbringing for who I am today. However, I am also fully aware of how religion can sometimes be used to oppress and exclude people who aren't "mainstream." Those who are marginalized, hidden away, and often ignored, such as people who are part of the LGBTQ community, cannot necessarily walk into a church in the black community on a Sunday morning and be accepted as-is. Oppression and exclusion doesn't just result in hurt feelings or a feeling of missing out; it can be dangerous, affecting mental health and self-esteem, and can result in loss of life.

When I got to high school, my brother and I joined the Lutheran church associated with the elementary school we attended. The transition was easy because we already knew the pastor, some of our schoolteachers also attended, and Mr. Coates the music teacher was the church's music director. The best part of church were the friends I made there and choir rehearsal every Thursday night. I loved to sing. I still do. It was so much fun learning the songs and how to sing my part. I was an alto, so I sat with the other alto ladies and we would harmonize with the sopranos and the tenors. Everyone was so nice and helpful. Some of the choir members would pick me up for rehearsal or drop me off afterwards because my parents still weren't churchgoers at that time. When I was pregnant with Andréa, the choir members even gave me a surprise baby shower. I was never made to feel ashamed for being a teen mother by anyone in the church.

All three of us, Andréa, my brother, and I would go to church together almost every Sunday. For Easter and Christmas Eve we'd dress up in our nicest outfits. Andréa was almost always in some big flouncy dress with patent leather shoes and tights. I would always pick a nice dress or suit to wear. Our hair would always be done up. Those were special times.

Despite being included, and the great times I had when singing in the choir, I often felt like an imposter. I never quite felt like I was Christian enough. Those feelings stem from the early days I spent in Sunday school across the street from my home and never went away. I perceived the other churchgoers as closer to God because they seemed very devoted and appeared to have a direct line to God, or at least I thought they did. I avoided leading prayer because I didn't think I could do it right. Others prayed so eloquently, using big flowery words and grand statements of faith and reverence. I just didn't have the vocabulary, so I stayed quiet. I felt less connected to God than I thought others felt. These judgments of myself bothered me a little. In hindsight,

I should have reached out to the pastor or a trusted elder about my thoughts and feelings for further guidance and instruction, but I didn't. I just pushed those thoughts and feelings away and continued to attend church until I ultimately had a shift in consciousness

Around 2008 I met a nice guy who turned out to be a lifelong friend. As my friendship developed with Chris Seals, he helped me to think very deeply about all sorts of things, one in particular being religion. One day we were having a deep conversation and he asked, "Do you believe the world was created in six days?" I paused, not sure how to answer his question. When I was young, my dad had a telescope and a book, *Atlas of the Night Sky*, with all the stars and constellations in it. He would sometimes take the telescope outside on our back porch at night and look at the stars. I knew that the sun was a star and that the earth was very old, and I could name all of the planets, but that was the extent of my understanding. I'm sure my father shared the big bang theory with me at some point, because he was a science aficionado, so I knew the scientific answer to my friend's question, but I also knew what the Bible said. I couldn't reconcile the two very different perspectives on such a simple question except to surmise that the biblical answer was the way that people of the time made sense of the world, so it wasn't wrong, it was just what it was! I couldn't give my friend a clear answer, though, and it bothered me.

He continued to ask questions that I didn't know the answers to. I was getting more and more defensive and a bit confused. Why didn't I know the answers to these questions? As a churchgoer, I felt like I was supposed to know this stuff, but I didn't. I had a Bible but didn't read it very often and I didn't go to Bible Study either. I quickly realized I didn't know as much as I thought I did.

He mentioned a book he'd read called *Conversations with God*. The author of the book was at a low point in his life and wrote an angry letter to God. He asked God why his life wasn't going as planned. When he was done, he sensed a presence or being that began to answer the questions and he wrote them down. The author then began asking other questions and that's how the book came to be. My friend mentioned an interesting part of the book about time being vertical instead of horizontal. That literally everything that had ever happened and is happening were occurring at the same time. I had never heard such a thing, but I was immediately drawn to this idea of the spiritual awakening the author had. My mind was blown.

I bought the book and read through it voraciously. There were many wonderful jewels in the book that still resonate with me to today. The first is that "we are all God." That literally, God is in everything and is everything. How liberating it must be to live without the idea that there is someone "up there," looking down and judging your every move, and is in anything and everything. I am sure we all would think and act differently towards ourselves and each other if we saw God in everything and everybody. Imagine how different our society would be! One of the main reasons that racism and other forms of oppression exist is because one group of people decides that another group of people hold less value. If God is in everyone, it would be impossible to assign less value to poor people, older adults, women, people with disabilities, or other groups that are often marginalized.

There was a catchphrase that gave me pause: "if you don't go within, you go without." In order to be fulfilled in life, you have to look within. Too often we look outside of ourselves for validation, for fulfillment, for answers. We don't stop and examine ourselves first. I loved the phrase so much I went to Color Me Mine many years ago and painted the sentence on a ceramic tile along with a big red heart with a hole in it and a shovel. That tile sits on my dresser in my bedroom as a reminder to always take care of myself first and the rest will fall into place.

I started to do more research, reading everything I could find. I learned how damaging and oppressive religion can be. By the time I'd finished reading all these materials, I decided that there was a higher power, a force or energy that was bigger than us all, but I couldn't say for sure what it was or what it was all about. As I began to think more deeply about what I believed and what was important to me, I decided to stay away from organized religion entirely.

"What happened?" my friend asked, shocked at my latest declaration. He had not intended for me to completely discard my beliefs. The book he gave me to read wasn't about that at all.

"Well, all of the questioning and thinking and reading helped me to start to question everything I've ever known, and so I decided to let go of all of it," I said.

What developed from this assertion is my personal belief system. There are two main paths at play. Energy does not die; it is simply transformed into something else. I believe that everyone is made up of two parts, their physical self and their spiritual self. When people die, their physical body is no longer here, but the spirit remains. How that spirit manifests itself is not entirely clear to me, but I believe that those manifestations can communicate with us in many ways.

People that I have physically touched who have since passed away have created pathways and opportunities for my growth and development. I am much more likely to think about my long-gone great-grandparents or my grandparents or recall experiences that I shared with them to gain strength and courage when I am going through a difficult time. These people held me in their arms and wished the best for my life and made sure that my family and I were safe. They left a legacy for my family and made sacrifices to ensure we were economically stable. They endured so much, traveled so far, and ventured into the unknown so that our lives would be better. How could I not look back at those people, who are no longer here, and not honor and respect them for what they did for me? My center, my core, the basis of everything that I am, resides with them and their parents, and their parents' parents. To me, believing in one

God in the traditional Christian sense would mean that my family and their time on this earth would be for naught, and I couldn't wrap my head around that possibility. A mentor I admire greatly, Marj Plumb, always says, "We stand on the shoulders on our ancestors." That phrase always touches me deeply and brings me to tears. I believe with my whole heart that my grandparents and great-grandparents continue to hold me up long after they are gone. They have left an amazing legacy for me and my family.

The book *Conversations with God* also states that there is no heaven and no hell. They are both here on earth. I am inclined to agree with that assertion. We all know someone right now living their own personal hell right here on earth, pulled down and oppressed by homelessness, violence, substance use disorder, stress, and any other "hell" that you can imagine. We don't need to die to experience our lowest of the lows. We also don't need to die to experience the best of humanity, the moments that make us feel most alive, the experiences that bring us together and remind us that we are more alike than we are different. All those things can and do happen in the here and now.

When the topic of religion comes up with black folks, they assume I believe what they believe, not once considering that I may have some other religious affiliation, or none at all. This is one of the reasons why I don't often speak about my thoughts on religion. I know that immediately I will be judged, which is ironic since the Bible speaks clearly on the importance of not being judgmental. To some extent, I understand the curiosity or the desire to assign value to my decision. If you've never been exposed to other belief systems or have been taught that other beliefs are invalid or subpar to your own, you'd never make the effort to learn about them and may even harbor negative feelings about the belief system and the people that practice it. It takes too much out of me to engage in explanatory conversations I'd rather not have with people who don't necessarily need to know where I stand. Instead, I keep my thoughts to myself, only sharing with my daughter or men I'm dating when the question inevitably arises. Deciding to keep my views about religion to myself can also be perceived as being unwilling or unable to accept other viewpoints, but since my views are not considered mainstream, I tend to avoid sharing to protect myself from misdirected criticism and conflict.

Had I not been open and receptive to thinking outside of my previous belief system, I may have not had such thoughtful and meaningful shifts in my consciousness. Because of my thoughtful and careful introspection, I continuously check myself, my biases, and my assumptions about others. In other words, my journey through religion and spirituality has helped me to be a better public health steward in my profession and community. I have immense respect for other cultures and have a keen interest in learning and understanding how other people live.

Another topic that always reminds me of how close-minded people can be is the ever-controversial topic of sexual health, specifically STD or HIV infection. My early work in public health provided me a very open, understanding, and nuanced perspective of these issues, which I know is a privilege. Not many people get accurate information on sexual health, reproductive health, and anatomy at home or in school, which leads to a lot of incorrect information being shared. Add to that the taboo surrounding sex, and the end result is avoidance, fear, and myths that lead people down a path of bad choices. One of the biggest issues currently is the decriminalization of HIV. Forty years after the start of the AIDS epidemic in the United States, legislators and HIV/AIDS experts are moving to remove many of the laws that made being HIV positive a crime. Unfortunately, public opinion lags behind the changing understanding of the virus and the resulting change in legislation. I witnessed an example of this recently on social media. My friend Dontá Morrison is a seasoned sexual health and HIV prevention expert and is very vocal about safe sex and healthy relationships. He posted an article on Facebook about an HIV-positive young man who infected several women he met through dating apps. Dontá's commentary about the incident is what set everybody off. He sympathized with the young women who got infected but pointed out that the responsibility of preventing HIV infection should be equally shared between both partners. It's not solely the responsibility of the HIV-positive person, who isn't even obligated to disclose his status. The response was swift and harsh. I expected some people to wrestle with this assertion, but I was shocked at how unyielding the opinions were. People could not see past their own limited understanding of HIV infection, which was largely inaccurate and based on stereotypes and half-truths. They were focused on who was right or wrong in the situation, not on the bigger picture, which was disease prevention. Many of the comments focused on how terrible the young man was to do such a thing, and not on the fact that the women had some responsibility to protect themselves. They couldn't see how important and empowering it is for people, especially women, to take ownership of their sexual health and not place their lives in someone else's hands, despite numerous experts (including myself) trying to clarify and explain. After all, regardless of who was at fault in the scenario, the women were negatively impacted by a decision that was made for them without their consent. The comments were disheartening. People questioned my friend's expertise, his profession, his job, and even his character. They were resistant to the information being shared because it called into question their understanding of sexual relationships, HIV infection, and human nature, and forced them to consider that what they knew to be true was not. The commenters thought the man had an obligation to disclose, that it was the right thing to do, and that he owed that to any sexual partner he had. They were placing a very high expectation on the infected person to disclose and no responsibility on the women, who should have some responsibility and accountability for their own health.

Ultimately, the lack of critical thought and failure to consider alternate points of view leads to demonization of our HIV-positive brothers and sisters and leaves them vulnerable to discrimination and violence.

When people experience problems in their personal or professional relationships, or witness something terrible happening in their communities, the first inclination is to figure out who's at fault or to pass judgment. More often than not, focusing on finding fault does nothing to fix the problem. It's very important to have a solution-focused mindset and work to find solutions to problems, not just argue about who's at fault, especially when the damage is already done. In most cases, it's infinitely more important to fix the problem than to worry about who caused it.

The other thing I see happening is tunnel vision, focusing in on one very specific part of a problem without understanding the complexities and nuances of the issue at hand. One very relevant example in my line of work is the debate on gun control. Violence of all kinds is a serious public health issue. When communities are impacted by violence, everyone suffers. Victims are the most visible, but those who witness violence are also greatly impacted and are often not counted or considered, especially if their wounds are not physical. The community also suffers economically. Investors typically abandon violent communities, leaving residents without resources and facilities that other communities can afford.

School mass shootings is one of the gun control debate issues that is a victim of the tunnel vision I described earlier. Many of us are begging for broader gun control laws to protect the most vulnerable of us, our children, and yet after every shooting, the focus is on either the shooter, or how to arm teachers, or bulletproof backpacks; all kinds of things to keep children alive except dealing with the root cause of the problem.

If we can't open our minds to other points of view, think critically about the issues, and find solutions to our problems, we will forever remain stuck where we are, a mindset very damaging to communities.

For many it can be the difference between life and death. Imagine a Muslim or transgender or gay patient attempting to seek medical care and being made to feel less than by their medical care provider, or even worse, given substandard treatment because of implicit (or explicit) bias. The patient may decide not to return because they sense that they are being treated poorly, but that's the least of our worries. They may decide to avoid medical assistance entirely because of that negative experience, increasing the likelihood of disease and shortened lifespan. It is not acceptable to allow personal beliefs to get in the way of providing care to patients or otherwise inhibit a person's ability to have access to resources and services that promote health. We are free to believe in who and what we choose, but it is so important for us, especially as women, to be open to other ideas and perspectives, especially when our beliefs marginalize and oppress other people. Women have the power to change social norms and influence others. Often what we say or do sets the standard for our families and our communities. We have a unique position to move our communities forward, but we must do it with an open mind, an open heart, and a desire to work towards finding viable solutions. The saying "if you're not part of the solution, you're part of the problem" is truer now more than ever.

Chapter Eleven

Open Your Eyes; Change Your Community

Public health is all around us. It touches every aspect of our lives. Important public health concepts impacted me as a child, in my role as a teen mom, in my romantic relationships, and as I continue to age. It's often said that when public health is working well, you don't see it. The system is like an invisible machine working in the background to keep communities healthy. I certainly didn't see it growing up. I had no idea what it was and how it worked until I became a teen mother and needed a way to earn a living and found myself working at a public health institution. When public health made itself known to me, the impact hit me like a ton of bricks. I am now a fierce public health advocate and a public health educator. Its main tenets of prevention and community stretch far beyond my place of employment, beyond "The Health Department" where I've spent the last fifteen years, and have become a part of who I am.

As much as I believe in the concepts and premise of public health, it's not perfect and could be much better. The public health system has been able to do quite a bit without a strong financial investment in prevention, but the lack of funding is egregious. Our society spends the most money of any developed country on medical treatments and procedures but spends very little money on prevention, which is ultimately more cost effective. This lack of funding results in outbreaks of diseases that we haven't seen in generations such as whooping cough and measles, infant mortality rates for black babies that are persistently high, and incidents of environmental injustice. Women have been at the forefront of all these very important issues, pushing for change at the community, organizational, and policy levels. We have been pushing for change regarding environmental issues in the low-income communities in LA surrounding the Exide battery factory, the Allen Co. oil drill site, and other environmental hazards across the county. We have been working with legislators to find ways to protect black women and their infants from implicit bias and other factors that lead to infant and maternal death. We have always stood up for our communities and will continue to do so, even when others have ignored the very real concerns from affected communities.

Years ago, in the early stages of my public health career, we spent a considerable amount of time teaching people to eat well and exercise, with the hopes that they would adopt these new behaviors and magically become healthier people. The problem with this strategy is that the societal structures that create the imbalance of power and privilege that create things like food swamps and poor park infrastructure still exist and continue to impact health in a negative way. One of the hardest pills to swallow as a black woman was coming to the realization that these same societal structures impact my health too! I am not immune to the structure just because I understand how it works. In many ways, understanding the issues has been hard for me because I see it in action everywhere. It can be quite dismaying to realize that my two college degrees and middle-class lifestyle might not be enough to protect ME from poor health and ultimately an early death. The current public health dialogue says that having a college education and being wealthy protects people from poor health. Those with more years of education, and a higher income, are less likely to engage in unhealthy behaviors like smoking, they are less likely to be obese, and are more likely to live longer than their less-educated counterparts. In a country like the United States, where everyone supposedly has full access to the American Dream, that information sounds great! If you go to school, work hard, and get a good job, not only will you benefit economically, you will more likely be healthier than those who don't. The problem is that this dream is unattainable for many people, particularly black people and other marginalized populations. If education, and all the resulting benefits of a good education, is supposed to provide a ticket to economic security and protect people from poor health, why is the infant mortality rate for babies born to college-educated black women higher than that of high-school-educated white women? If education is supposed to protect people from bad health, why isn't it enough to protect me as an educated black woman? Further, why has the education system, and the other institutions we interact with regularly, failed black people so that it is virtually impossible for us to improve our social and economic standing overall, which would ultimately improve our health as well?

It is easy to declare a community disadvantaged or troubled, or to write off entire groups of people as bad or undesirable because they don't speak our language, or look like us, or live and love the way we do. Most of us live our lives in neat little boxes, rarely stepping outside of them to see what else is it out there. When we rarely step out of our boxes and only see life in one very prescriptive way, our opinions about life are short sighted. How can we care about the LGBTQ community, or homeless families, or incarcerated individuals, or children living in poverty if we've never taken the time to understand them, to talk to them about life as they see it? We often push our narrow perspective and opinions on people, which can have life-threatening impacts on them. The terrible thing is that since everyone is used to living in their neat box, they perceive their experience to be the norm, and superior to other experiences. We dismiss them and tell them that what they experience isn't so, because we are uncomfortable with their reality. It forces us to come to terms with what we believe to be true, which causes people to become defensive and even more stubborn in their thought process. Many people live happily in the silent majority, remaining in that little box at the expense of others who are suffering. I see this happening with women in many situations. Some of us are quick to defend behaviors and actions that tear down other women. I have witnessed women defend physical and sexual abuse towards girls and other women to preserve relationships with partners and spouses; tear down pregnant and parenting teens; dismiss women who are part of the LGBTQ community; and either actively participate in the adultification of our young girls or do nothing while it happens. To be fair, women who tear down their colleagues are victims of the very same system that perpetuates the abuse and harm of girls and women. We have to help them heal as well, or else they will pass down those qualities to the next generation, but we also have to protect and stand up for those who are vulnerable and cannot speak for themselves. It is our responsibility to do so.

The hard part is to take the time and do the work to uplift and empower others who differ from you. It's easy to encourage and uplift our friends and family who look like us and walk the same paths we do. We have to shift the narrative and help people understand that when we take care of the least of us, we take care of all of us. The overweight child or teenager needs encouragement and love, not embarrassment and body shaming. Teen mothers need a strong support system, resources, and the wisdom of other community members, not judgment.

Public health has to keep everyone safe by anticipating health threats and also work on heavy-hitting topics such as racism and health equity. Despite the large amount of responsibility and the many difficulties faced, there have been tremendous gains over the years. Life expectancy rates have increased tremendously over the decades. The shift in focus towards what are called "upstream" issues gives public health professionals the ability to address the causes of disease disparities at their root and look for solutions that can create lasting change in communities.

Although many public health issues are abstract and quite complex, we as women have a huge responsibility to create the healthy communities that we want to thrive in. More often than not, we are looking for someone or something to fix our plight, but it really begins in our homes, our schools, and on our streets. We all know the system is rigged and favors those who have resources and privilege, but it does not help us to wait for someone to come save us. Each of us has immediate power, the ability to do a thing, anything, to create positive impact in our communities. It could be mentoring young people, opening a business and hiring local residents, teaching a skill, or sharing resources. Your contribution does not have to be grandiose; you do not have to be a martyr. We all have something to offer to improve our collective well-being. I have seen women gather together other women in the community to build stronger partnerships and mentorships. There are women in my city who are business owners who help others start their businesses. I know young women engaged in work that uplifts community, engages young people, and brings community together. What drives them all is passion, ambition, and a desire to help. There is space for all of us to do this work to build each other up and grow healthier, stronger communities.

I try to practice what I preach regarding creating positive change. I am a teacher, a mentor, a connector, and a creator. I understand all too well that it can't just be about me and what I want or how I envision the world. I must consider others with different experiences and different perspectives all equally valid, and all worthy of being heard. There are times that I wonder if what I'm doing is worth it, if it even resonates with folks, or if I've crossed the line and said something a bit too far off in left field. I have my hand in so many things. My plate is always full with teaching, working my day job, and blogging, so it can be difficult for me to step back and see the scale of all that I'm working on and the value of the work. I'm always reminded that I'm on the right path. On many occasions a student or a colleague will say that they were feeling the exact same thing that I mentioned but didn't know how to put it into words or share that I am who they aspire to be. Every so often someone will stop me in person, send me an email, or reach out to me via social media to tell me how proud they are of me. I'm always humbled and a bit shocked by those messages because I honestly don't think I'm doing anything special. I'm just doing what I truly feel led to do.

Everything in life is connected. Nothing happens in isolation. If one person is impacted, we are all impacted. It is very easy for us to see an incidence of violence, natural disaster, or some other tragedy and think, "that happens to those people over there on that side of town," and it's not true. For example, we often hear the story that the growing homeless population has to do with the large number of people who come to Los Angeles from other parts of the world and end up unemployed and on the streets. The data doesn't that support that notion. The majority of homeless in Los Angeles are our neighbors, our friends, our family. They are us. The same is true regarding discussions around violence and trauma. People often think low-income communities are the most impacted by the effects of violence, but studies indicate that a good number of people across all socioeconomic lines have experienced trauma due to negative experiences during childhood and have very real negative health effects because of those experiences. We have to realize that we are more alike than we are different. I have been grateful to learn this firsthand through the many relationships I've developed with people from all different backgrounds over the years. Once you sit and just talk to people, you realize that many of your struggles are theirs as well.

The question that is most important now is: How do we talk about these issues in a way that makes sense to communities? It can be very upsetting to realize that for the most part, many of the things that impact health are out of the direct control of most people.

How do we create change in communities?

1. **Shift your thinking.**

   As I said earlier, when something isn't right, the first inclination is to look externally for the answer to the problem. In communities, looking externally means waiting for an authority figure of some sort to create or change a law or enact some other type of action to fix the issue. I challenge you to shift your thinking and consider actions you can take to become the solution in your communities. There is nothing that says we have to wait for permission to act to create change. We have immediate and collective power to shift things right now.

2. **Think about what your talents are and use them as leveraging point to move things forward.**

   My professional background is in public health but I use my love of fashion and beauty to push the concepts of both body positivity and supporting local businesses. Use your platform to push your message. If you like to cook, hold cooking classes. Use what you know and share it with others. This helps to foster a sense of community, which is very important in improving health.

3. **Just start.**

   You don't have to do this big production to have an effect in the community. You don't even have to have a lot of money or a lot of free time. Nipsey Hussle, a well-respected and loved rapper and businessman in my community, embodied the concept of starting small. He spent lots of time on the corner of Crenshaw and Slauson, not far from where I live, selling his music. He would later own property on that same corner and begin many more business ventures before his untimely death at age thirty-three. Don't wait for some huge moment to begin because it might never come. Start by thinking of what it is you have to offer and begin sharing it with others. I have a love for supporting local businesses owned by black women. My very small way of supporting their work is by hosting pop-up shops in my backyard and inviting friends to come by and support. I didn't wait for more popularity or exposure to start the pop-ups. I just started.

4. **Look for like-minded people**.
   Find folks who are interested in what you do and want to see their communities in a better place. Ask them questions, share resources, collaborate. Don't worry about the people you think should be supporting you. Focus on finding the people who will support you and your efforts.

5. **Remember that you are not alone in your situation or thinking.**
   Ask for support from those close to you. Tell them when you need help. If you don't have a support system, create one. There are community organizations that are great for connecting with people. Also, social media is a wonderful place to find groups of people who share common interests.

In 2018, I finally got my chance to talk about my concerns publicly. I've wanted to do a TED talk ever since I saw Dr. Nadine Burke Harris give a talk highlighting the significance of childhood trauma on health. I received a request for submission announcement via email for a TEDx Occidental College event. I was so excited and knew immediately what my talk would focus on. Everything I was feeling about the racial equity training at work was fresh on my mind, and I began to think about how those feelings impacted how I teach. I also wanted to focus on how important my status as a black woman is on my students, and how the connections between my lived experience and teaching style amplify the experiences I provide my students. I excitedly submitted my TEDx talk proposal and waited to hear if I was selected. As soon as I heard that I was selected to speak, I drafted my speech and enlisted the help of a good friend. She is a member of Toastmasters and used her public speaking expertise to help me create a series of "stories" that conveyed the message I wanted to share. I learned very quickly that the "stories" were very important; it would be nearly impossible to memorize the speech. Focusing on the stories helps the speech to be conveyed in a natural manner, and once the key points of the story are committed to memory, remembering each word becomes less important. For weeks I practiced my talk. First I used index cards to help me remember each story. As I got more familiar with the content, I was able to connect each story together. The hardest part was remembering the transitions, but soon enough, I was able to give my TEDx talk without the help of notes. I was ready!

My lived and professional experience, coupled with my social justice work, has a great impact on how I do almost everything in life. It shapes my thoughts and actions and even impacts the way I teach. At that racial equity training that made me so upset, I was reminded that diversity and representation is important in the workplace, in academia, in politics, pretty much everywhere. A former professor once said to me,

"If you're not at the table, you're on the menu." It means if you're not part of the group making the important decisions, more than likely the results will negatively impact you. My work is about me AND bigger than me, all at the same time. I will always be a public health advocate because helping communities acquire the resources and information needed to live healthier lives is important to me. However, I realize now that my work is much broader. I have a responsibility to share what I've learned along the way to inspire more change in the South Los Angeles community that I love.

Self-Care and Stress Reduction

Push **past your fears and "do it anyway."** When you are poor, you don't have the opportunity to unwind. Vacations and such are for those who have the privilege of disposable income and paid time off. For most of my life, travel was the furthest thing from my mind. At the age of eighteen, during my first semester in college, I became a mother. I was more concerned with trying to finish school, working, and raising my daughter. I didn't realize it then, but there is privilege in being able to travel, to see how others live, and to marvel at the beauty of the world outside of your immediate community. Travel felt foreign—unattainable both financially and socially for a young black girl from South Los Angeles in the late 1990s. As a child, the farthest my family traveled was Lake Mead just outside of Las Vegas, a four-hour drive from our home. I have fond memories of our old wood-paneled station wagon packed with a cooler full of snacks and the radio on full blast. Even those short trips to Vegas to a two-bedroom, two-bathroom mobile home owned by my great-grandparents were a privilege that escaped many people in my community.

As a college student I'd eavesdrop on my classmates who talked about trips they'd taken to far-off places over breaks and how much fun they'd had. The places they described were so different from my gritty little corner of the world. I could never relate to their experiences. My family was lower middle class; there simply wasn't enough money for my parents to send me anywhere.

If I were to be completely honest, my daughter and money weren't the only reasons that I stayed so close to home. A lingering doubt in the back of my mind, a feeling of uncertainty and outright fear overwhelmed me about the idea of going too far afield. I got anxious on short flights and wasn't sure how I would fare on an international flight, flying for a dozen hours or more. As a plus-size black vegan, I had lots of other things to ponder. Would I fit comfortably in an airplane seat? Would I be able to eat the food on the flight? Would I be stared at like some sort of sideshow curiosity by the locals? What if there was nothing to eat when I got there? Even the idea of being outside of the United States worried me a bit. Even though I'm normally a rational and grounded person, I couldn't seem to stop thinking of worst-case scenarios. I had a hard time wrapping my head around the idea of my life post-travel, not quite convinced I'd make it back.

All these fears gave me the opportunity to reflect. I realized that many of them were inherited from my mother. Although I had managed to avoid internalizing most of the worries she'd projected onto me over the years, I could not shake the feeling that something really terrible could happen to me if I went too far from home. At the core of my stress was the loss of control that this trip would force me to face. Unlike so much of my life up until then, I would be flung into totally unfamiliar territory. For many, this is what makes travel exciting, and for some this is what makes travel debilitating. I had to grapple with the fact that I was one of the latter.

Beyond fear, there were no real barriers to making my travel dream a reality. My daughter was now an adult, my income had significantly increased over the years, and I had time to explore unchartered waters. This important benchmark mattered to me.

So, even though I neither knew the first thing about planning a trip out of the country nor did I even really know where I wanted to go, I got a passport. Luckily, I have a group of sister friends and colleagues who are avid travelers. They offered their advice and suggestions: first, pack noise-cancelling headphones, a tablet full of downloaded movies and music, and a travel pillow. Second, don't fall sleep right away because it will make the flight seem longer. Third, watch two or three moves, sleep for several hours, and then watch two more movies to help the time pass quickly. And fourth, get anti-anxiety meds from my doctor.

One friend had just returned from a girls' trip to Greece organized by a black-owned travel agency called PushPin Adventures. She shared how incredible the experience had been and mentioned they were planning a trip to Thailand. She encouraged me to sign up.

Before I could talk myself out of it, I went online and quickly set up my payment plan for the trip.

My friends were ecstatic when I told them I was going. Inevitably they'd ask if I was excited as well. The answer, for a very long time, was "no." My fears had blocked my excitement. I didn't even share my exciting news with anyone in my family other than my daughter. As the trip grew closer, the fear grew ever more present. I had gotten all the comforting words I was going to get from others. I had to give myself the rest. I realized that the only way to get over it was to go through it. I had to do it for myself, even if I honestly thought I wouldn't make it back home.

Finally, the time arrived for me to head to the airport. My bags were packed and ready to go. I had my passport in hand. My daughter came by to wish me safe travels. My boyfriend chatted me up as we headed off to the airport, his way of helping me take my mind off the trip (and I was grateful for it!). We only had a few moments to exchange hugs before I jumped out of the car, grabbed my suitcase, and ran into the terminal. Once inside I took everything in. Little time was allowed to be scared or anxious because there were many airport instructions to follow, so many lines to stand in.

Before I knew it, I was on the plane. I fit into my seat and felt entirely comfortable asking for a seatbelt extender. It can be a bit unsettling being plus-size and traveling so I was grateful that there were no problems fitting in the seat. I heeded every tip I'd been given and was able to manage the thirteen-hour flight from Los Angeles to Xiamen, and then onto Bangkok with no problems.

The trip was life changing. I got to take in intricate artwork in Bangkok and Phuket, tried durian for the first time (I hated it), and even got to feel like a queen for a day when we went to a tailor to have some things made to fit our bodies perfectly. Some of my fears did materialize. There was an incident in Phuket where other tourists tried to take pictures of us without permission, but we handled it swiftly. Vegan options were scarce, but I made it work with rice and vegetable dishes. And I seriously wondered if I would survive the hour-long rocky boat ride to the Phi Phi Islands, but I did.

My story shows you that not everyone who goes abroad is the stereotype of the intrepid globetrotter. Some of us use travel as an opportunity to address deep-seated fears and to improve our mental health. The fear of the unknown can hold us captive to what's familiar and safe. I faced my fears and in return I got the chance to see how other people live, experience a new culture, and make twenty-two new friends in the process. This trip pushed me to see what I am capable of. It taught me that I can both be afraid of an experience and move forward with making it happen at the same time. And the trip reminded me that I can still surprise myself—even at forty.

As women we have an amazing talent; the ability to merge our intellect and insightfulness with our hearts. We can be incredibly passionate and emotional about what is important to us, and yet temper it with knowledge and experience to bring about change. We are also nurturers, taking the time and effort to build up others until they can flourish on their own. We have to continue to flex our heart power and build up our insightfulness and our sense of kinship. It's the only way that we will grow and our communities will improve.

After working in the same office for almost a decade, I promoted three times within a two-year timeframe. It was a huge professional victory for me. Since 2014, I had applied for a couple of jobs and was told by HR that I didn't meet the minimum qualifications. It was upsetting because I was already doing the work! I was clearly qualified. While bothered, I didn't let it get me down.

Applying for these promotions showed me I needed help. I was happy with my current job but wanted to promote to a high-level position one day and was having trouble imagining how I would get there. My friends—whom I named the "Fabulous Sistafriends of South LA," women of color I met through work in the community over the last decade (directors of community-based organizations, policy directors, consultants, high-level executives at national reproductive health organizations, and public health nurses)—offered to help think through it with me. How could I say no? All of us have graduate degrees, and two of us have doctorate degrees. They came over one Sunday morning with breakfast snacks, chart paper, and markers, and helped me strategize what to do with my career and the steps I could take to reach my dream job. When those positions reopened, I applied again. Suddenly I was highly qualified although my education and experience had not changed. It was a miracle, but I think it was also the power of those women holding me up. I keep one of the rejection letters on my desk to remind me of the importance of trying again, of being persistent, of knowing and valuing my education and experience, and most importantly, of advocating for self. I learned that no one can stand up for me better than I can, that no one can want success for me more than I want it for myself, and that I will never place my future, personally or professionally, in the hands of someone else.

I have been blessed to have a career that is fulfilling and personal and professional relationships that have improved my life tremendously. If you find yourself in a space where work does not fulfill you and your relationships aren't supportive, here are three suggestions to empower you:

1. Talk to people who are doing what you want to do. I always tell students or recent graduates to go on informational interviews and talk to people who are doing the work. This advice works well for anyone looking to change careers or needing insight into next steps in their current career. Any good professional will be more than happy to share their experience and perspective and offer advice.

2. Find a mentor or other like-minded individuals who have the same vision and goals. In my case, my mentors were former supervisors or colleagues who had reached a place in their professional lives that was inspiring to me.

3. Always be prepared. When I realized I was talking to the founder of a program that I was interested in at that party the mayor hosted, I was ready to talk about my personal and professional experience and share my interest in the program. As the saying goes, "If you stay ready, you won't have to get ready."

The passion that I apply to my work in public health stems from my gratitude for the honor and privilege of working many years in the community that I live in. Although I am fortunate to draw a salary doing what I love for my community, you can look at your own neighborhood and find small yet significant areas that you can improve with like-minded individuals. Some of the best examples of community change come from one or two individuals who came together to solve a problem the community was having. I show up every day in love with public health and an advocate for women of color and anyone else who is marginalized. I get to use my voice to help others, to solve important public health issues, and to change my little corner of the universe.

I will never forget how uncomfortable I felt sitting in that training, hearing the data about people I see in my community every day. I have since learned that growth occurs during the most uncomfortable moments in our lives. When life gets awkward, feels weird, and is downright strange, a metamorphosis is happening. If we stay the course to see those challenging moments through, growth will inevitably occur. Change won't happen overnight, and limbo is never pretty, but the results are life changing.

The most important part in making it through the discomfort is doing all you can to reach back and lift up your sisters, your friends, and those who need help and support as they make their own way, chart their own course through the discomfort. We have to act as guides to those that need us most, shining light along the way, steering them through the rough patches, helping them figure out what is real and what is not so that they can also transform themselves. They in turn will act as guides for the next generation and so on and so on.

We all have our own journey, but my cautionary tales and determination can save you from some unnecessary heartache and pain. You are not alone in finding your own personal sense of community and vigilance about heath. I never believed my mother when she told me there was nothing new under the sun. I was absolutely certain that she didn't understand me or know what I was going through. Now that I'm a mom I realize how wrong I was. Although there may be some subtle differences in experiences, we can all find a common thread of relatability, which is to live long, healthy lives, and be afforded the same services and privileges as our neighbors. When we allow ourselves the time to open up to each other and share, we can lean on each other and grow stronger from our experiences.

Over the last twenty-plus years, I have remained in a state of self-exploration, sometimes as a mother, other times with love (of self and others), in successes and failures. You are capable of the same level of inspiration and motivation to create positive transformational change in your community. You do not have to be a professional in public health, have any strong political ambitions, or have my skin color. All of us have more power than we realize to be a positive force in the lives of others. We live alongside each other. We are in the community. From there, we can rise up and be the change. Start where you are, with what you have, and you can create community, foster relationships, and become a part of the solution. It really does start with you!